Highlights: AN ILLUSTRATED HISTORY OF ART

Highlights · AN

ILLUSTRATED HISTORY OF ART

EVERARD M. UPJOHN

Columbia University

JOHN P. SEDGWICK, Jr.

University of North Carolina, Greensboro

HOLT, RINEHART AND WINSTON

New York • Chicago • San Francisco • Toronto • London

April, 1966

PREFACE

THIS BOOK is designed specifically as a supplementary text for courses in art history and criticism. Although clearly useful for the survey course, the book, in our experience, should be useful as well for period courses. In addition, we should like to think that the book as a whole tells a pictorial story worth following for its own sake.

We have elected to put considerable emphasis on major periods, key types of monuments and works of art, "high" styles, and crucial artists. Certain personal predilections for the use of details, or the inclusion of drawings and prints, have for the most part been sacrificed to the greatest possible inclusion of significant whole works in architecture, sculpture, and painting. The decorative arts have had to be passed by.

Wherever possible, without sacrificing the individual significance of works of art elsewhere, we have tried to represent material to be found in American museums and collections, especially in major metropolitan areas. We have followed the principle that photographic reproductions are of value chiefly for review, and that when the original can be consulted this value is augmented.

The book as a whole seeks to balance the disparate demands of range and inclusiveness with sufficient size of reproduction that the work can be perused clearly. With more inclusions, the size might have suffered from the "postage-stamp" appearance; with fewer, the range of the book would have suffered. Furthermore, there are certain advantages in having an average of five reproductions on a page. Various comparisons, sometimes two- and three-way comparisons, illustrating both visual and historical points, are thus made possible.

A book of this sort poses enormous and continuing problems of availability and quality of reproductions. It can never be precisely what its authors would like it to be, but rather the best compilation they can present when faced with such decisions as that between an inferior reproduction of a preferred work and a better reproduction of a work that, though adequate, is not quite the one desired. In certain instances, inevitably, permission is not forthcoming; in others, available photographs are too sorry to warrant reproduction.

Professor Upjohn selected the photographs, and wrote the captions, for all sections except those dealing with sculpture and painting of the Western world from the Etruscan period to the present.

Our heartfelt thanks are due to Professor Allan S. Weller, University of Illinois, to Mr. H. H. Arnason, Vice-President for Art Administration, The Solomon R. Guggenheim Foundation, to Professor David R. Coffin, Princeton University, to Mr. John Canaday, *The New York Times,* and to Thomas M.

Folds, Dean of Education, The Metropolitan Museum of Art, New York, for their constructive criticism of the subjects chosen for illustration.

We wish to express gratitude and appreciation to Esther Gist of the publisher's staff for patient, tireless, and cooperative assistance.

E.M.U.
J.P.S.

Acknowledgments

For the reproductions we are indebted to museums, private collectors, publishers, and photographic agencies far too numerous to list here in detail. Special acknowledgment, though, is made to the following for their more than generous permission to use the photographs: Fratelli Alinari, Florence; The Art Institute of Chicago; The Baltimore Museum of Art; F. Bruckmann Kg., Munich; Caisse Nationale des Monuments Historiques, Paris; The French Embassy (French Cultural Services) and the French Government Tourist Office, New York; The Frick Museum, New York; The Italian State Tourist Office and the Italian Information Center, New York; The Solomon R. Guggenheim Museum, New York; The Louvre, Paris; The Metropolitan Museum of Art, New York; The Museum of Fine Arts, Boston; The Museum of Modern Art, New York; The National Gallery, London; The National Gallery, Washington, D.C.; The Nelson Gallery of Art and Atkins Museum, Kansas City; The Pennsylvania Academy of Fine Arts, Philadelphia; The Philadelphia Museum of Art; Spanish National Tourist Bureau, New York; and Dr. F. Stoedtner, Düsseldorf, and Dr. Konrad Prothmann, Baldwin, L.I.

A Note on the Abbreviations

In an effort to conserve space for larger reproductions we have used abbreviations.

Arch. Photo.	Caisse Nationale des Monuments Historiques, Paris
BIS	British Information Services, New York
DIS	Danish Information Services, New York
EMU	Everard M. Upjohn
ESTA	Egyptian State Tourist Administration, New York
FGTO	French Government Tourist Office, New York
GITO	Government of India Tourist Office, New York
GTIO	German Tourist Information Office, New York
Ist. Ital. Cult.	Istituto Italiano di Cultura (Italian Information Center), New York
ISTO	Italian State Tourist Office, New York
ITIO	Italian Tourist Information Office (Italian Information Center), New York
MFA	Museum of Fine Arts, Boston
MMA	The Metropolitan Museum of Art, New York
MOMA	The Museum of Modern Art, New York
NIO	The Netherlands Information Service Office (NIS), New York
NPS	National Park Services, Washington, D.C.
OTIO	Official Tourist Information Office, The Hague
SNTO	Spanish National Tourist Office, New York
YSTO	The Yugoslav State Tourist Office, New York

CONTENTS

Highlights: AN ILLUSTRATED HISTORY OF ART

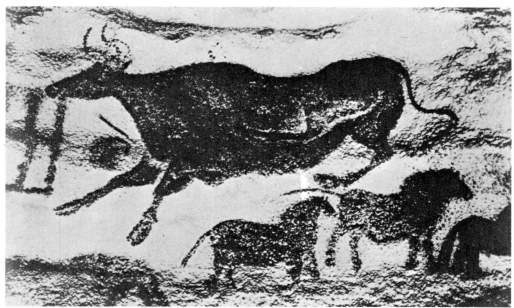

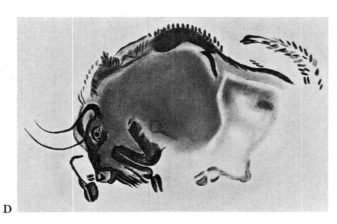

A.   Lespugue Statuette. Mus. de l'Homme, Paris.
B.   Woolly Mammoth (*c*. 15,000 B.C.). *c*. 1′8″ wide. Font-de-Gaume. *(Mus. de l'Homme)*
C.   Animal Group (*c*. 12,000 B.C.). 5′ 6″ wide. Lascaux. (Maringer and Bandi, *Art in the Ice Age*, Praeger)
D.   Bison (*c*. 12,000 B.C.). 4′ 9″ wide. Altamira.
E.   Reindeer and Salmon (*c*. 12,000 B.C.). Lorthet *(Am. Mus. Nat. Hist.)*

A.   Group of Archers (*c.* 7000 B.C.). 3' 10" high. Valltorta Gorge. (Maringer and Bandi, *Art in the Ice Age,* Praeger)
B.   Salisbury Plain, Stonehenge (*c.* 2000–1500 B.C.). 25' high. *(Mus. de l'Homme)*
C.   Stonehenge, restored. *(Stoedtner)*
D.   Sakkara, Pyramid of Zoser (*c.* 2980–2700 B.C.). 197' high. *(ESTA)*
E.   Gizeh, Pyramids (*c.* 2700–2600 B.C.). Great Pyramid, 479' high, 767' wide. *(ESTA)*
F.   Typical Mastabas.

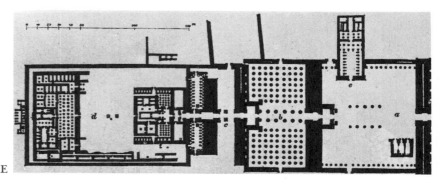

A.   Gizeh, Temple of the Sphinx (*c.* 2700–2600 B.C.). Monoliths, 13′ 6″ high. *(Stoedtner)*
B.   Beni Hasan, Tomb of Khnumhotep (*c.* 1900 B.C.). *c.* 28′ wide. *(Stoedtner)*
C.   Karnak, Temple of Khons (*c.* 1200 B.C.). 105′ x 225′. *(Stoedtner)*
D.   Luxor, Temple of Amon Ra, hypostyle hall (*c.* 1300 B.C.). *(ESTA)*
E.   Karnak, Temple of Amon Ra, plan (*c.* 1900–*c.* 200 B.C.). 1220′ x 338′. *(Stoedtner)*
F.   Karnak, Temple of Amon Ra, hypostyle hall, model (*c.* 1300 B.C.). Central columns, 69′ high, 12′ diameter. Metropolitan Mus. Art, New York. Bequest of L. H. Willard, 1883.

A.   Deir el-Bahri, Mortuary Temple of Queen Hatshepsut (*c.* 1480 B.C.). Columns, 14′ 6″ high.
B.   Edfu, Temple of Horus, pylon (237–212 B.C.). *c.* 250′ x 145′. *(Stoedtner)*
C.   Edfu, Temple of Horus, seen from pylon. *(Stoedtner)*
D.   Sphinx, Gizeh (*c.* 2700–2600 B.C.). Total height, 66′. *(Stoedtner)*
E.   Kaaper, "Sheikh el Beled" (*c.* 2700–2600 B.C.). 3′ 7″ high. Nat. Mus., Cairo. *(Stoedtner)*
F.   Khafre, detail (*c.* 2700–2600 B.C.). Complete figure, 5′ 6″ high. Nat. Mus., Cairo. *(Stoedtner)*

A

B1

2

C

D

E

A.   Ranefer (*c.* 2500 B.C.). 5′ 11″ high. Nat. Mus., Cairo.
B (1 and 2).   Rahotep and Nefert (*c.* 2700–2600 B.C.). 3′ 11″ high. Nat. Mus., Cairo. *(Stoedtner)*
C.   Seated Scribe (*c.* 2500 B.C.). 21″ high. Louvre *(Arch. Photo.)*
D.   Sesostris I (*c.* 1900 B.C.). Berlin. *(Stoedtner)*
E.   Ikhnaton (*c.* 1360 B.C.). 2′ 1″ high. Louvre. *(Arch. Photo.)*

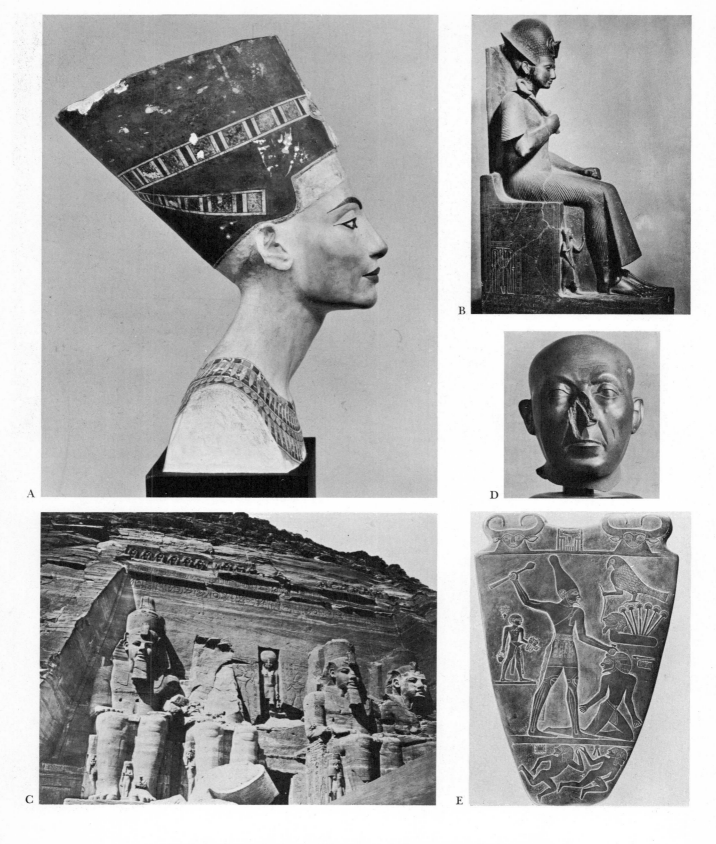

A.   Nefertiti, reproduction (*c.* 1450 B.C.). *c.* 1′ 8″ high. MMA, Rogers Fund, 1925.
B.   Ramses II (*c.* 1250 B.C.). 6′ 4″ high. Turin. *(Stoedtner)*
C.   Abu Simbel, Temple of Ramses II (1257 B.C.). Colossi, 55′ high. *(Stoedtner)*
D.   Head of a Priest (4th century B.C.). 4″ high. The Mus. Fine Arts, Boston.
E.   Palette of King Narmer (*c.* 2900–2800 B.C.). 25½″ high. Nat. Mus., Cairo. *(Photo of cast, MMA, Purchase, 1930)*

A.   Sakkara, False Door of Neferseshemptah (c. 2500 B.C.). (Stoedtner)
B.   Panel of Hesire (c. 2700 B.C.). 3′ 9″ high. Nat. Mus., Cairo.
C.   Seti I Offering to Osiris (c. 1300 B.C.). Abydos.
D.   Geese of Medum (c. 2700 B.C.). Nat. Mus., Cairo. (Arch. Photo.)
E.   Brickmaking (c. 1800 B.C.). Tomb of Rekhmere. (Stoedtner)

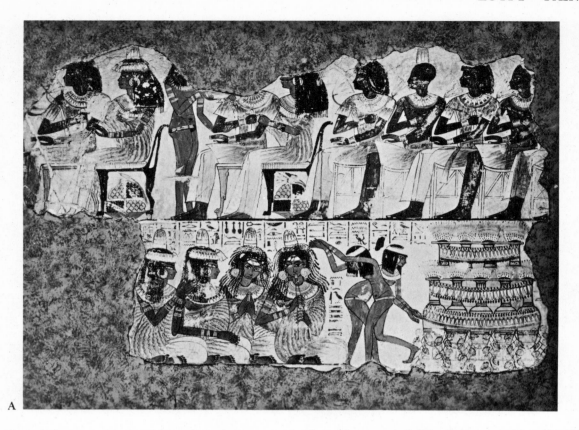

A

B

C

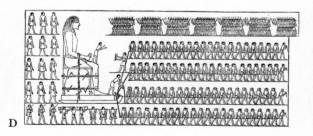

D

A.   Banquet Scene (*c.* 1400 B.C.). Brit. Mus., London.
B.   Thebes, Tomb of Nakht, Chapel (*c.* 1450 B.C.). Real wall, 55″—63″ wide. (*MMA, photo Henry Burton*)
C.   Fowler Hunting in a Marsh (*c.* 1300 B.C.). Figure, 2′ 10″ high. Brit. Mus.
D.   El Bersheh, Moving a Colossus (*c.* 1800 B.C.). *Perrot and Chipiez*, I, 527)

A

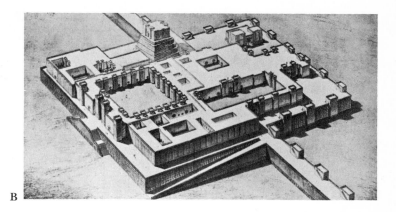

B

C

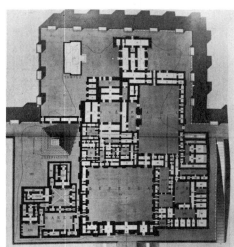

D

E

F

A. Ziggurat. *(Stoedtner)*
B. Khorsabad, Palace of Sargon, restored. *(Stoedtner)*
C. Khorsabad, Palace of Sargon, interior. *(Stoedtner)*
D. Khorsabad, Palace of Sargon, plan (722–705 B.C.). 1050′ x 1140′.
E. Babylon, Gate of Ishtar (*c.* 575 B.C.). Relief of lion, 6′ 5″ x 3′ 6″. *(Stoedtner)*
F. Winged Bull, Palace of Ashurnasirpal, Nimrud (885–860 B.C.). 10′ 2″ x 2′ 2″ x 10′ 3″ high. MMA, Gift of J. D. Rockefeller, Jr., 1932.

A.   Head of God Abu, Tell Asmar (3000–2340 B.C.). Full figure. 30″ high. Orient. Inst., U. of Chicago. *(Pub., Vol. 44,*
U. of Chicago Press)
B.   Gudea of Telloh (*c.* 2400 B.C.). 1′ 5″ high. Louvre.
C.   Ashurnasirpal (885–860 B.C.). 3′ 4″ high. Brit. Mus. *(Stoedtner)*
D.   Stele of Ur-nina (*c.* 3100 B.C.). 1′ 6″ wide. Louvre. *(Arch. Photo.)*
E.   Stele of Naram-sin (*c.* 2300–2200 B.C.). 6′ 6″ high. Louvre. *(Arch Photo.)*

A.   Stele of Hammurapi (*c.* 1775 B.C.). 2′ 4″, height of relief. Louvre. (*Arch. Photo.*)
B.   Ashurnasirpal Storming a City, from Nimrud (885–860 B.C.). 3′ high. Brit. Mus.
C.   Ashurnasirpal Hunting Lions, from Nimrud (885–860 B.C.). 3′ high. Brit. Mus.
D.   Ashurbanipal Feasting from Nineveh (668–626 B.C.). 4′ 5″ wide. Brit. Mus.
E.   Wounded Lioness, from Palace of Ashurbanipal, Nineveh (668–626 B.C.). 25″ x 40″. Brit. Mus.

A.   Pasargadae, Tomb of Cyrus (*c.* 530 B.C.). Interior, 10′ x 7′. *(Stoedtner)*
B.   Persepolis, Apadana of Xerxes (*c.* 465 B.C.). *(Orient. Inst., Chicago)*
C.   Persepolis, Gate of Xerxes (486–465 B.C.). *(Stoedtner)*
D.   Bactrians Leading a Camel, Palace of Xerxes, Persepolis (486–465 B.C.). 3′ high.
E.   Lion Attacking a Bull, Palace of Xerxes, Persepolis (486–465 B.C.). *(Iran Embassy)*
F.   Double Bull Capital, Susa, Palace of Artaxerxes (404–358 B.C.). 10′ high. Louvre. *(Arch. Photo.)*

A

B

C

D

E

F

A.   Ctesiphon, Taq-i-Kisra (A.D. 242–272). 312′ x 112′. *(Stoedtner)*
B.   Peroz I Hunting (A.D. 457–463). Diameter, 8½″. MMA, Fletcher Fund, 1934.
C.   Investiture of Ardashir, Naqsh-i-Rustam (A.D. 224–241). *(Stoedtner)*
D.   Knossos, Palace (*c.* 1800–1600 B.C.). 400′ square. (*Brit. School of Archaeology at Athens*)
E.   Knossos, Palace, reconstruction. *(Stoedtner)*
F.   Knossos, Palace, restored stair well. (*Royal Greek Embassy*)

[1] For Islamic Persia, see Pl. 57-59.

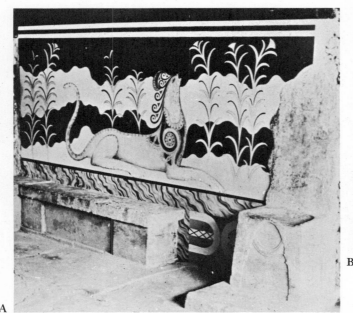

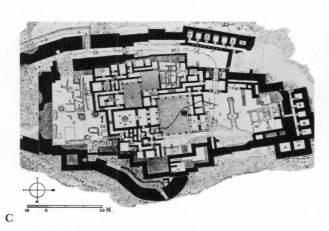

A.   Knossos, Palace, Throne Room, restored (*c.* 1800–1600 B.C.). (*BIS*)
B.   Tiryns, Palace, reconstruction. (*Stoedtner*)
C.   Tiryns, Palace, plan (1500–1100 B.C.). *c.* 480′ x 310′. (*Stoedtner*)
D.   Mycenae, Treasury of Atreus, section (*c.* 1250 B.C.). 48′ 6″ diameter. (*Stoedtner*)
E.   Mycenae, Lion Gate (*c.* 1250 B.C.). Relief, 9′ 6″ high. (*Staat. Bild., Berlin*)

A

B

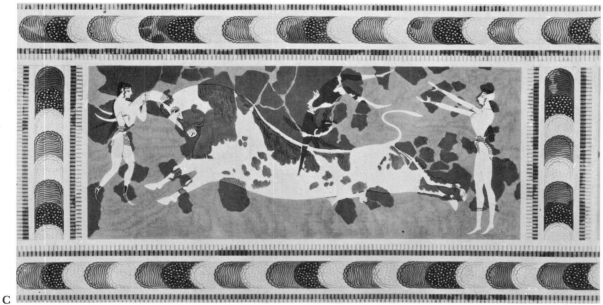

C

D

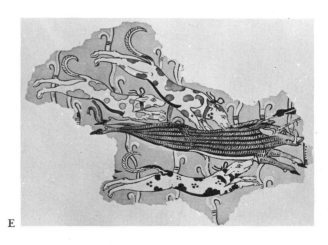

E

A. Snake Goddess (*c.* 1600 B.C.). 6½" high. MFA.
B. Sarcophagus, from Hagia Triada (*c.* 1400 B.C.). 8½", height of figures. Heraklion Mus., Crete.
C. Bull Leapers, from Palace at Knossos (*c.* 1800–1600 B.C.). 5′ 3″ wide. Heraklion Mus., Crete.
D. Cat Stalking a Pheasant, from Hagia Triada (*c.* 1700–1580 B.C.). 1′ 9″ high. Heraklion Mus., Crete. *(Stoedtner)*
E. Boar Hunt, from Tiryns (1300–1200 B.C.). 1′ 5″ wide. Nat. Mus., Athens. *(Stoedtner)*

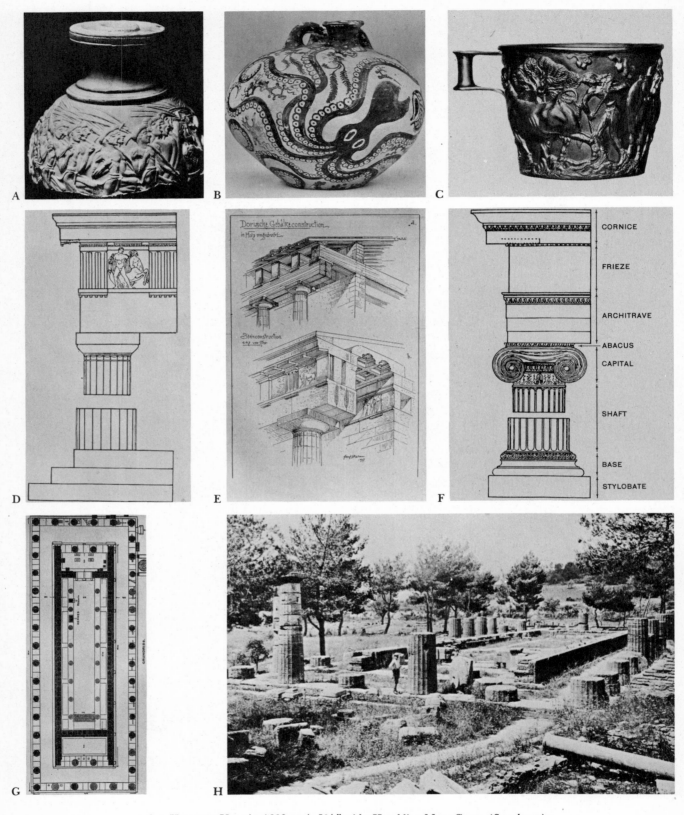

CORNICE

FRIEZE

ARCHITRAVE

ABACUS

CAPITAL

SHAFT

BASE

STYLOBATE

A.   Harvester Vase (*c.* 1600 B.C.). 5½″ wide. Heraklion Mus., Crete. *(Stoedtner)*
B.   Octopus Vase, from Gournia, reproduction (*c.* 1500 B.C.). 8″ high. MMA, Dodge Fund.
C.   Gold Cup, from Vaphio (1500–1100 B.C.). 3″ high. Nat. Mus., Athens.
D.   Doric Order.
E.   Doric Order, hypothetical origin in wood construction. (J. Durm, *Baukunst der Greichen*)
F.   Ionic Order.
G.   Olympia, Heraeum, plan (*c.* 590 B.C.). 61′ 6″ x 164′ 1″. *(Stoedtner)*
H.   Olympia, Heraeum. *(Stoedtner)*

A.   Corinth, Temple of Apollo (*c.* 540 B.C.). 70′ 6″ x 176′ 11″. *(Stoedtner)*
B.   Athens, Acropolis, reconstruction. *(Stoedtner)*
C.   Delphi, Treasury of the Siphnians (530–525 B.C.). 20′ 1½″ wide.
D.   Paestum, Temple of Hera, interior (*c.* 460 B.C.). Temple, 197′ x 80′; column diameter, *c.* 3′. *(Alinari)*

A

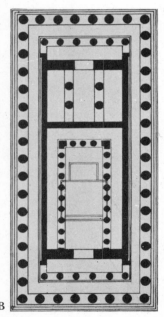

B

C

D

A.   *Ictinus* and *Callicrates*, Athens, Parthenon (447–432 B.C.). 101' x 228'.
B.   Athens, Parthenon, plan.
C.   Athens, Parthenon, showing horizontal curvature.
D.   Athens, Parthenon, interior, from model. MMA, Purchase 1890, Levi Hale Willard Bequest.

A

B

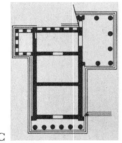

C

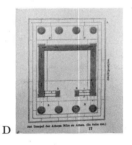

D

E

A.   Athens, Erechtheum, north porch (421–405 B.C.). 35′ 2″ wide. *(Stoedtner)*
B.   Athens, Erechtheum, south porch. *(Stoedtner)*
C.   Athens, Erechtheum, plan.
D.   Athens, Temple of Wingless Victory, plan.
E.   Athens, Temple of Wingless Victory (427–424 B.C.). 17′ 9″ x 26′ 10″. *(Alinari)*

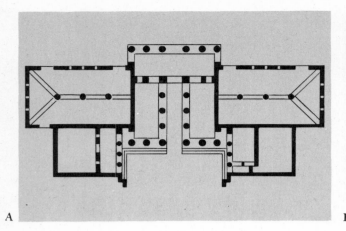

A. *Mnesicles.* Athens, Propylaea, plan (437–432 B.C.). Central portico, 69′ wide.
B.   Athens, Propylaea, west side. *(Stoedtner)*
C.   Epidaurus, Tholos, after Thiersch (*c.* 360–320 B.C.). *c.* 65′ diameter. *(Stoedtner)*
D.   Epidaurus, Tholos, Corinthian capital. 2′ 1½″ high. *(Stoedtner)*
E.   Halicarnassus, Mausoleum, after Adler (*c.* 350 B.C.). *c.* 86′ x 106′. *(Stoedtner)*
F.   Athens, Choragic Monument of Lysicrates (334 B.C.). 54′ high. *(Royal Greek Embassy)*

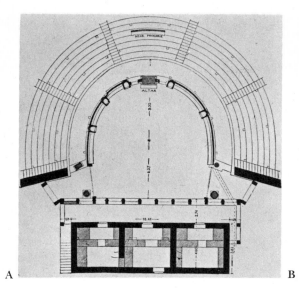

A

B

C

D

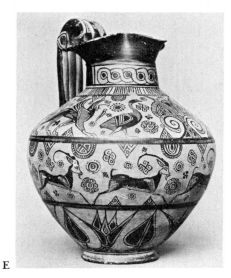

E

F

A.   Priene, Theater, plan, after Borrmann (*c.* 300 B.C.). *(Stoedtner)*
B.   Epidaurus, Theater (*c.* 350 B.C.). 387′ diameter. *(Stoedtner)*
C.   Pergamum, Altar of Zeus (197–159 B.C.). 119′ 6″ x 112′ 3″. *(Stoedtner)*
D.   Attic Vase, geometric style (*c.* 750 B.C.). 42½″ high. MMA, Rogers Fund.
E.   Rhodian Vase (7th century B.C.). 12¼″ high. MFA.
F.   *Clitias* (6th century B.C.). François Vase, black-figured style. 2′ 1″ high. Archaeolog. Mus., Florence. *(Stoedtner)*

A

B

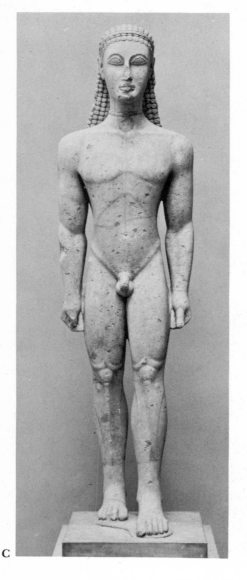

C

D

E

A. *Exekias* (*fl.* 6th century B.C.). Dionysus, black-figured style (*c.* 530 B.C.). Diameter, 12″. Munich.
B. *Euphronius* (*fl.* 6th century B.C.). Hercules and Antaeus, red-figured style (*c.* 500 B.C.). Louvre.
C. "Apollo," from Attica (*c.* 600 B.C.). 6′ 1″ high. MMA, Fletcher Fund.
D. "Apollo," head.
E. Chares of Branchidae (late 6th century B.C.). 4′ 10″ high. Brit. Mus. *(Stoedtner)*

A   B   C   D

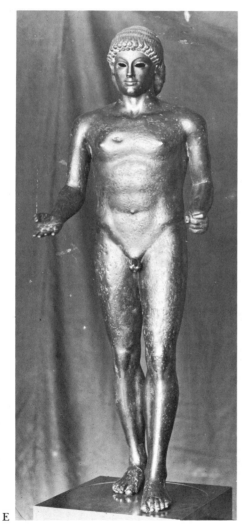 

E   F

A.   Calf Bearer (*c.* 570 B.C.). 5′ 5″ high. Acropolis Mus., Athens.
B.   "Apollo," from Tenea (*c.* 550 B.C.). 5′ high. Glyptothek, Munich.
C.   Statuette from Ligurio (*c.* 460 B.C.). 5″ high. Berlin. (*Stoedtner*)
D.   Nikandra, from Delos (7th century B.C.). 5′ 9″ high. Nat. Mus., Athens. (*Stoedtner*)
E.   "Apollo" Piombino (5th century B.C.). 3′ 9″ high. Louvre. (*Arch. Photo.*)
F.   Hera of Samos (*c.* 550 B.C.). 6′ high. Louvre. (*Arch. Photo.*)

A.   Perseus Slaying Medusa; Heracles and the Cecropes, from Temple C, Selinus (550–530 B.C.). 3′ 9″ x 4′ 11″. Palermo. (*Stoedtner*)
B.   Stele of Aristion (*c.* 515 B.C.). 5′ 9″ high. Nat. Mus., Athens. (*Stoedtner*)
C.   *Antenor* (*fl.* late 6th century B.C.). Maiden from the Acropolis. Acropolis Mus., Athens. (*Stoedtner*)
D.   Relief from Pharsalos (6th century B.C.). 2′ 2″ wide. Louvre. (*Arch. Photo.*)
E.   Seated Gods, frieze, Treasury of the Siphnians, Delphi (550–520 B.C.). 25″ high. Delphi.
F.   *Micciades* and *Archermus*. Nike of Delos (550–520 B.C.). 3′ high. Nat. Mus., Athens. (*Stoedtner*)

A

B

C

D

A.   East Pediment, restored, Temple of Aphaia, Aegina (*c.* 495–485 B.C.). 45′ wide.
B.   Athena and Warriors, west pediment, Temple of Aphaia, Aegina. Athena, 5′ 6″ high. Glyptothek, Munich.
C.   Wounded Warrior, west pediment, Temple of Aphaia, Aegina. Height of head, 18″. Glyptothek, Munich.
D.   Head of Fallen Warrior, east pediment, Temple of Aphaia, Aegina. Glyptothek, Munich.

A

B

C

D

E

A.   *Critius* and *Nesiotes.* Harmodius and Aristogiton (478 B.C.). 6′ 1″ high. Nat. Mus., Naples. *(Alinari)*
B.   Charioteer (*c.* 470 B.C.). 5′ 11″ high. Delphi.
C.   Charioteer, head. (*Royal Greek Embassy*)
D.   *Myron* (*c.* 490–430 B.C.). Discobolus, reconstruction. *c.* 4′ 6″ high. (*Stoedtner.*)
E.   *Paeonius* (5th century B.C.). Victory. 7′ 1″ high. Olympia.

A

B

C

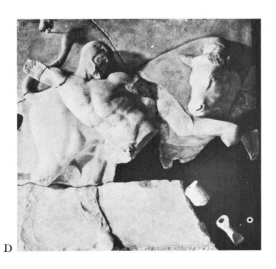

D

E

A.   West Pediment, restored, Temple of Zeus, Olympia (468-460 B.C.). 91′ wide. *(Stoedtner)*
B.   Apollo, west pediment, Temple of Zeus, Olympia. Complete figure, *c.* 10′ high. Olympia. *(Stoedtner)*
C.   Centaur Biting a Lapith, west pediment, Temple of Zeus, Olympia. 6′ 8″ high. Olympia. *(Stoedtner)*
D.   Heracles and the Cretan Bull, metope, Temple of Zeus, Olympia. Complete metope, 5′ 3″ high x 5′ wide. Olympia. *(Stoedtner)*
E.   Birth of Aphrodite, Ludovisi Throne (*c.* 470 B.C.). 4′ 8″ wide. Nat. Mus., Rome. *(Alinari)*

A.   Slaughter of the Niobids, red-figured style (460–450 B.C.). Height of band, *c.* 10″. Louvre. (*Arch. Photo.*)
B.   Lekythos, white-ground vase, Athenian (*c.* 440 B.C.). 13½″ high. MFA.
C.   *Phidias* (*c.* 500–430 B.C.). Athena Lemnia (*c.* 450 B.C.). 6′ 6″ high. Head, Bologna; body, Dresden.
D.   *Phidias.* Athena Parthenos (438 B.C.). Varvakeion copy. Original statue, 39′ high. Nat. Mus., Athens. (*Stoedtner*)
E.   Athena Parthenos, detail, Strangford Shield. Brit. Mus. (*Stoedtner*)
F.   Athena Lemnia, head. Bologna.

A.   Centaur and Lapith, metope, Parthenon, Athens (447–432 B.C.). 3′ 11″ x 4′ 2″. Brit. Mus. (Stoedtner)
B.   Centaur and Lapith, metope, Parthenon. Brit. Mus. (Stoedtner)
C.   Horsemen, frieze, Parthenon. 3′ 4″ high. Brit. Mus. (Stoedtner)
D.   Chariot Group, frieze, Parthenon. Brit. Mus. (Stoedtner)
E.   Seated Gods, frieze, Parthenon. Brit. Mus. (Stoedtner)

A

B

C

D

A.   East Pediment, restored, Parthenon, Athens (447–432 B.C.). *c*. 90′ wide.

B.   "Theseus," east pediment, Parthenon. 5′ 8″ long. Brit. Mus.

C.   "Demeter, Persephone, and Iris," east pediment, Parthenon. Persephone, 3′ 4″ high. Brit. Mus. *(Stoedtner)*

D.   "The Three Fates," east pediment, Parthenon. Left figure, 3′ 4″ high. Brit. Mus.

A. Caryatid, from Erechtheum, Athens (421–405 B.C.). 7′7″ high. Brit. Mus. *(Stoedtner)*
B. *Polyclitus* (*fl.* 450–420 B.C.). Doryphorus. 6′ 6″ high. Nat. Mus., Naples. *(Alinari)*
C. *Polyclitus.* Diadumenos. *c.* 6′ high. Brit. Mus. *(Stoedtner)*
D. Stele of Hegeso (*c.* 420–410 B.C.). 4′ 11″ high. Nat. Mus., Athens. *(Stoedtner)*
E. *Praxiteles* (*fl. c.* 390–330 B.C.). Aphrodite of Cnidus. 6′ 8″ high. Vatican, Rome. *(Stoedtner)*
F. *Praxiteles.* Satyr, "Marble Faun." 5′ 7″ high. Capitoline Mus., Rome. *(Stoedtner)*

A

B

C

D

E

G

A. *Praxiteles (fl. c.* 390–330 B.C.). Hermes Carrying the Infant Dionysus. 6′ 11″ high. Olympia. *(Stoedtner)*
B.   Hermes, head. Olympia. *(Stoedtner)*
C. *Praxiteles.* Apollo Sauroktonus. 5′ high. Louvre. *(Arch. Photo.)*
D. *Scopas (fl. c.* 390–340 B.C.). Meleager. 3′ 10″ high. Fogg Mus., Cambridge, Mass.
E. *Scopas.* Head, from the Temple of Athena Alea, Tegea (370–355 B.C.). *c.* 10″ high. Nat. Mus., Athens. *(Stoedtner)*
F.   Charioteer, from a frieze of the Mausoleum, Halicarnassus (*c.* 350 B.C.). 2′ 10″ high. Brit. Mus. *(Stoedtner)*

A.   Amazon Frieze, from Mausoleum, Halicarnassus (c. 350 B.C.). 2′ 11″ high. Brit. Mus. *(Stoedtner)*
B.   Demeter of Cnidus (c. 340–330 B.C.). 5′ high. Brit. Mus. *(Stoedtner)*
C.   Niobid Chiaramonti (4th century B.C.). 5′ 9″ high. Vatican. *(Stoedtner)*
D.   *Lysippus* (*fl. c.* 370–325 B.C.). Agias. 6′ 5″ high. Delphi. *(Stoedtner)*
E.   *Lysippus.* Apoxyomenos. 6′ 9″ high. Vatican. *(Stoedtner)*
F.   Mourning Women Sarcophagus, from Sidon (c. 350 B.C.). 8′ 8″ long. Ottoman Mus., Istanbul. *(Stoedtner)*
G.   Alexander Sarcophagus, from Sidon (c. 330 B.C.). 10′ 5″ long. Ottoman Mus., Istanbul. *(Sabah)*

A.   Dying Gaul, Pergamum (*c.* 225 B.C.). 3′ high. Capitoline Mus.
B.   Gaul Killing Himself and His Wife, Pergamum. 6′ 11″ high. Terme Mus., Rome. *(Stoedtner)*
C.   Dying Gaul, back of A. *(Alinari)*
D.   Head of Gaul, detail of B. *(Stoedtner)*
E.   Zeus Group, from Altar of Zeus, Pergamum (197–159 B.C.). 7′ 6″ high. Berlin. *(Stoedtner)*
F.   Athena Group, from Altar of Zeus, Pergamum. 7′ 6″ high. Berlin. *(Stoedtner)*

A

B

C

D

E

F

A.   Demosthenes (3rd century B.C.?). 6′ 9″ high. Vatican. *(Stoedtner)*
B.   Aphrodite of Melos (3rd–2nd centuries B.C.). 6′ 8″ high. Louvre. *(Arch. Photo.)*
C.   Victory of Samothrace (*c.* 200 B.C.), 6′ 6″ high. Louvre. *(Arch. Photo.)*
D.   Apollo Belvedere (late 4th century.). 7′4″ high. Vatican. *(Stoedtner)*
E.   Venus de Medici (3rd century B.C.?). 5′ high. Uffizi, Florence.
F.   Aphrodite from Cyrene (1st century B.C.?). 5′ high. Terme Mus.

A.   *Boëthus* (*fl.* 2nd century B.C.). Boy with a Goose. 2′ 9″ high. Munich.
B.   Farmer Driving His Bull to Market (1st century B.C.). 11″ x 12″. Munich. *(Stoedtner)*
C.   Old Market Woman (2nd century B.C.). 4′ 1½″ high. MMA.
D.   *Agesander, Polydorus,* and *Anthenodorus* of Rhodes. Laocoön (*c.* 40 B.C.). 7′ 11″ high. Vatican. *(Alinari)*
E.   Tanagra Figurines (late 4th century B.C.). MMA, *left,* Rogers Fund, 1906; *center and right,* Gift of J. Pierpont Morgan, 1917.
F.   Laocoön, detail. *(Stoedtner)*

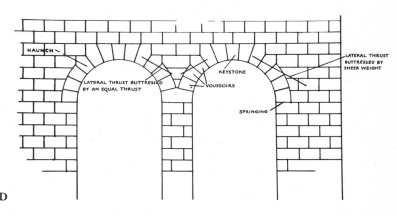

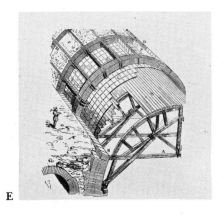

A. Boxer (*c.* 50 B.C.). 4′ 2″ high. Terme Mus. *(Alinari)*
B. Archaistic Athena (1st century B.C.). Nat. Mus., Naples. *(Alinari)*
C. *Menelaus* (*fl.* 1st century B.C.). Orestes and Electra. Terme Mus. *(Alinari)*
D. Structure of an Arch. EMU.
E. Barrel Vault Construction. (Viollet-le-Duc, *Discourses on Architecture,* Grove reprint, 1959)
F. Etruscan Temple, reconstruction. (Anderson, Spiers, and Ashby, *Architecture of Ancient Rome,* plate VIII)

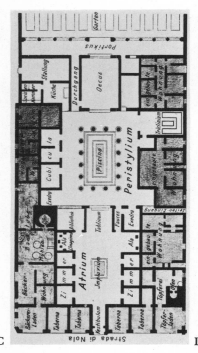

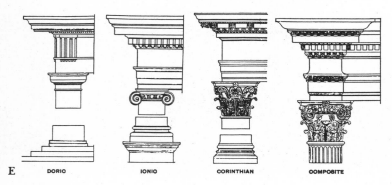

A.   Nîmes, Pont du Gard (*c.* A.D. 150). Total length, 902′; total height, 161′.
B.   Segovia, Aqueduct (*c.* A.D. 100). 94′ high, 900′ long. *(SNTO)*
C.   Pompeii, House of Pansa, plan (*c.* A.D. 50). 319′ x 124′. *(Stoedtner)*
D.   Pompeii, House of Vettii, peristyle (*c.* A.D. 50). 85′ x 55′. *(Alinari)*
E.   Roman orders.
F.   Nîmes, Maison Carrée (16 B.C.). 49′ x 84′ x 56′ high.

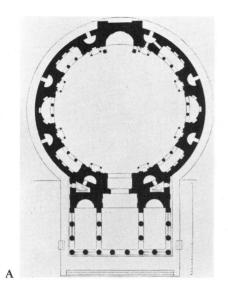

A

B

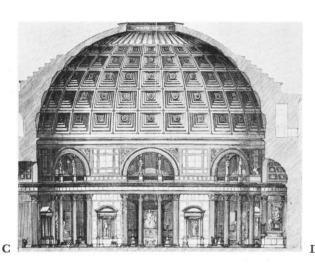

C

D

E

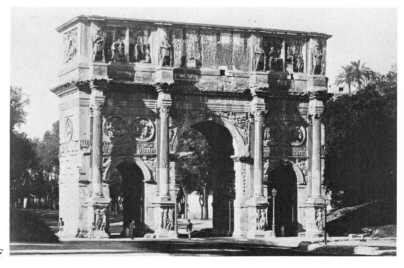

F

A.   Rome, Pantheon (A.D. 120–124; portico, 27 B.C.). Interior diameter, 142′. *(Stoedtner)*
B.   Rome, Pantheon. Portico, 108′ wide.
C.   Rome, Pantheon, section. *(Stoedtner)*
D.   Rome, Pantheon, interior. *(Stoedtner)*
E.   Rome, Arch of Titus (A.D. 70–81). 43′ 8″ wide x 47′ 4″ high. *(Stoedtner)*
F.   Rome, Arch of Constantine (A.D. 312). 82′ wide, 67′ 7″ high. *(Stoedtner)*

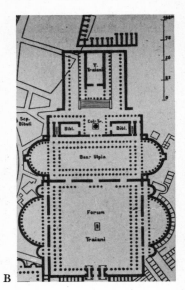

A.   Rome, Forum, restored by Tognetti. *(Stoedtner)*
B.   Rome, Forum of Trajan (A.D. 113). *c.* 920′ x 620′. *(Stoedtner)*
C.   Rome, Colosseum (A.D. 70–80). 620′ x 513′ x 157′ 6″ high. *(Ist. Ital. Cult.)*
D.   Rome, Colosseum, interior restored. *(Stoedtner)*
E.   Nîmes, Amphitheater (A.D. 1st–2nd centuries). 435′ x 345′ x 70′ high.

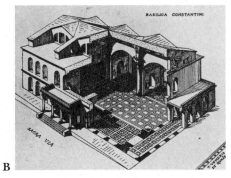

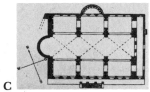

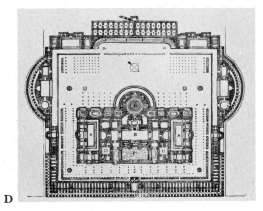

A.   Orange, Theater (A.D. 2nd century). Stage wall, 121′ high. *(Stoedtner)*
B.   Rome, Basilica of Constantine, reconstruction (A.D. 310–313). 195′ x 265′. *(Stoedtner)*
C.   Rome, Basilica of Constantine. *(Stoedtner)*
D.   Rome, Baths of Caracalla (A.D. 211–217), plan. Central building, 750′ x 380′.
E.   Rome, Baths of Caracalla, interior restored. Central hall, 183′ x 79′ x 108′ high.

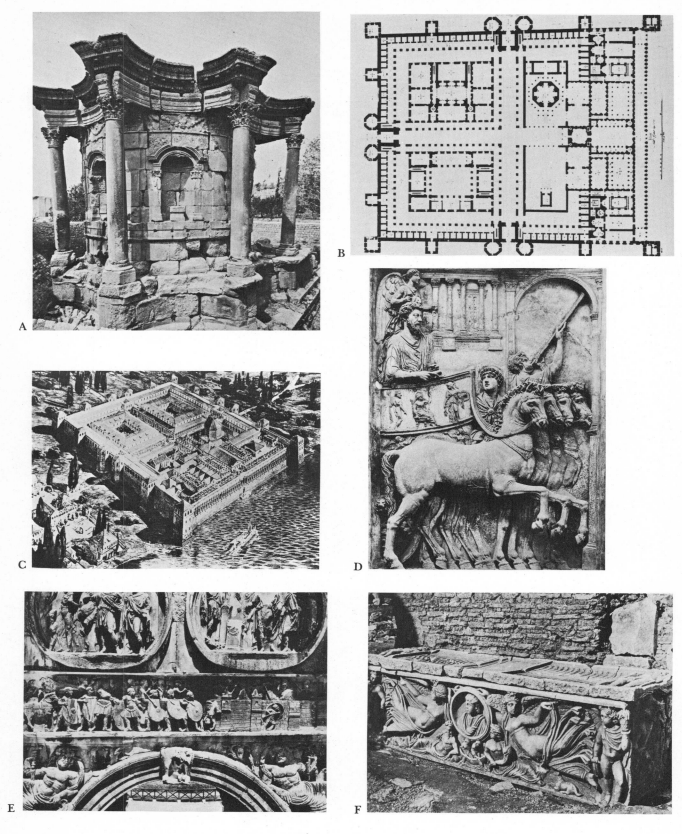

A.   Baalbek, Round Temple (A.D. 2nd century). 64' extreme diameter. *(Stoedtner)*
B.   Spalato, Palace of Diocletian (A.D. 284–305). 592' x 698'. *(Stoedtner)*
C.   Spalato, Palace of Diocletian, reconstruction. *(YSTO)*
D.   Triumphal Entry of Marcus Aurelius (A.D. 161–180), relief. Capitoline Mus. *(Stoedtner)*
E.   Rome, Arch of Constantine (A.D. 312), south side, detail. Commemorative relief. *(Stoedtner)*
F.   Sarcophagus. *(Stoedtner)*

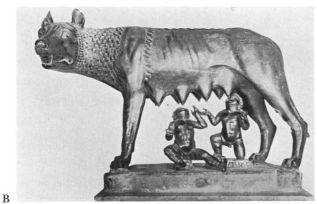

A.   Tomb, reclining couple (late 6th century B.C.). 79″ long. Villa Giulia Mus., Rome. *(Arch. Photo.)*
B.   She-wolf (5th century B.C.). 52″ long. Capitoline Mus.
C.   Chimera from Arezzo. Archaeolog. Mus., Florence. *(Stoedtner)*
D.   Apollo of Veii (6th century B.C.). 68″ high. Villa Giulia Mus. *(Phototeca)*

A

B

C

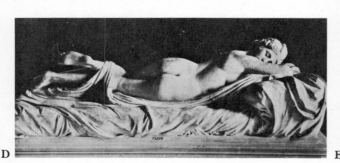

D

E

A.   Augustus, from Prima Porta (*c*. 10 B.C.). 7′ 3″ high. Vatican. *(Stoedtner)*
B.   Etruscan Orator (150 B.C.). 71″ high. Archaeolog. Mus., Florence *(Alinari)*
C.   Equestrian Statue of Marcus Aurelius (A.D. 161–180). *c*. 9′ 10″ high. Campidoglio, Rome. *(Stoedtner)*
D.   Hermaphrodite. *c*. 69″ length. Villa Borghese, Rome. *(Stoedtner)*
E.   Trajan Sails from Ancona. *c*. 49″ high. Column of Trajan, Rome. *(Alinari)*

A.   Unknown Roman. Dresden. *(Stoedtner)*
B.   Agrippina. Nat. Mus., Naples. *(Stoedtner)*
C.   Mosaic of Musician. Pompeii. *(Stoedtner)*
D.   Sacrifice of Iphigenia. Casa del Poeta Tragico, Pompeii. *(Stoedtner)*

A

B

C

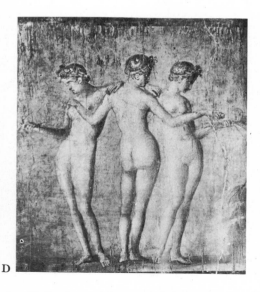

D

E

A.   Wall painting (Roman period, 1st century B.C.). Villa at Boscoreale. 8′ high. MMA, Rogers Fund, 1903.
B.   Dionysus and Ariadne. House of Vettii, Pompeii. *(Stoedtner)*
C.   Mythical Marriage of Dionysus to Ariadne. Villa dei Mysteri, Pompeii. *(Stoedtner)*
D.   Three Graces, a painting from Pompeii. Nat. Mus., Naples. *(Stoedtner)*
E.   Wall Painting. Villa dei Mysteri, Pompeii. *(Stoedtner)*

A

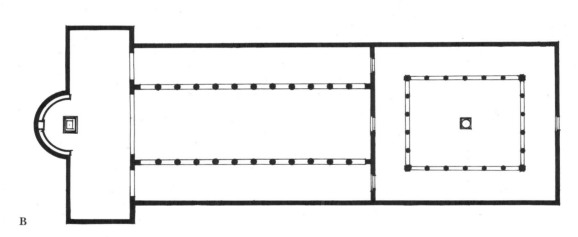

B

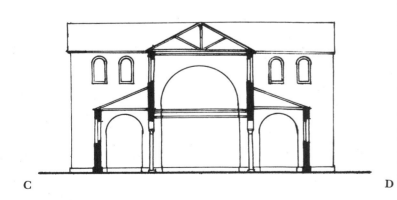

C

D

A.   The Battle of Issus, between Darius and Alexander (c. 100 B.C.). 10½′ long. Nat. Mus., Naples.
B.   Early Christian Basilica, typical plan. EMU.
C.   Early Christian Basilica, typical section. EMU.
D.   Rome, San Lorenzo, F.L.M. Portico, 75½″ wide. (Stoedtner)

A.   Rome, San Lorenzo, F.L.M., nave (1216–1227). Central aisle, 36′ wide.
B.   Rome, San Lorenzo, F.L.M., presbytery (578). Central aisle, 36′ wide. *(Alinari)*
C.   Rome, Santa Sabina, nave (425). Central aisle, 43′ wide. *(Alinari)*
D.   Rome, San Clemente, nave (1084–1108). Nave and apse length, 129′; nave width, 35′.
E.   Rome, San Clemente, atrium. Columns, 14′ high.
F.   Rome, Santa Costanza (323–337). Dome diameter, 70′. *(Alinari)*

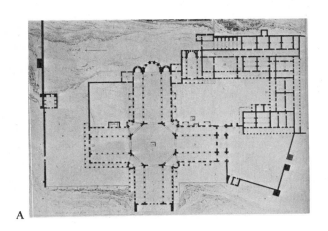

A. Kalat Seman, St. Simeon Stylites (5th century). 315' x 318' *(Stoedtner)*
B. Tourmanin, Basilica, restored (6th century). *(Stoedtner)*
C. Kalb Louzeh, Basilica (6th century). Nave and aisles, 50' wide.
D. Ravenna, Tomb of Galla Placidia (*c.* 440). 49' x 41'.
E. Ravenna, Tomb of Galla Placidia, interior. *(Stoedtner)*
F. Ravenna, Sant' Apollinare Nuovo, interior (549). *(Stoedtner)*

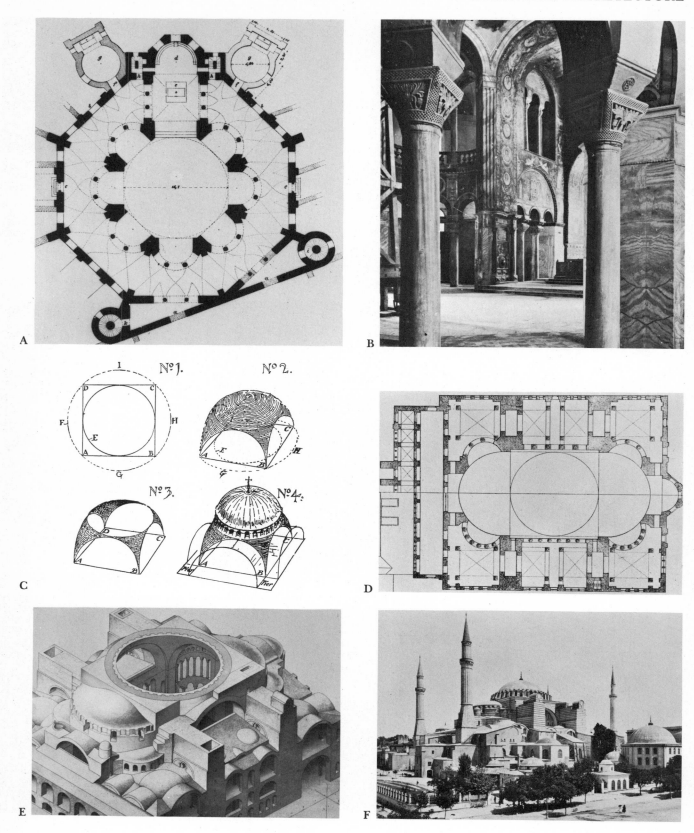

A.   Ravenna, San Vitale (526–547). Diameter, 112'. *(Stoedtner)*
B.   Ravenna, San Vitale, interior. *(Stoedtner)*
C.   Dome on Pendentives.
D.   *Anthemius of Tralles* and *Isidorus of Miletus*. Constantinople, Hagia Sophia (532–537). 308' x 236'. *(Stoedtner)*
E.   Constantinople, Hagia Sophia, dissection.
F.   Constantinople, Hagia Sophia, exterior. 183' 9" high.

A

B

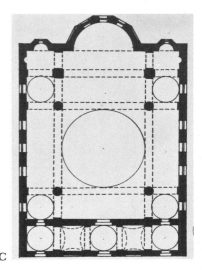

C

D

E

F

A. Constantinople, Hagia Sophia, interior.
B. Constantinople, Hagia Sophia, detail. *(Stoedtner)*
C. Typical Byzantine Plan, Second Golden Age. EMU.
D. Achtamar, Church (915–921). Total width, 44'. *(Stoedtner)*
E. Daphni, Monastic Church (11th century). 47' x 67'. *(Stoedtner)*
F. Daphni, Monastic Church, interior. Dome, 24' diameter. *(Royal Greek Embassy)*

A

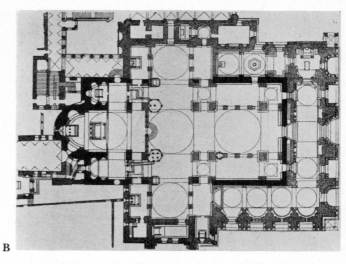

B

C

D

E

F

A.   Athens, Little Metropolitan Church (12th century). 38' x 25'. *(Stoedtner)*
B.   Venice, St. Mark's (1063). 249' x 168'. *(Stoedtner)*
C.   Venice, St. Mark's, exterior. *(Stoedtner)*
D.   Venice, St. Mark's, interior. *(Alinari)*
E.   Manassia, Church (1407).
F.   Chernigov, Cathedral of the Transfiguration (1017). 122' x 126'. *(Trudy,* XIV, Mosk. Arkheolog. Obshch., 1908)

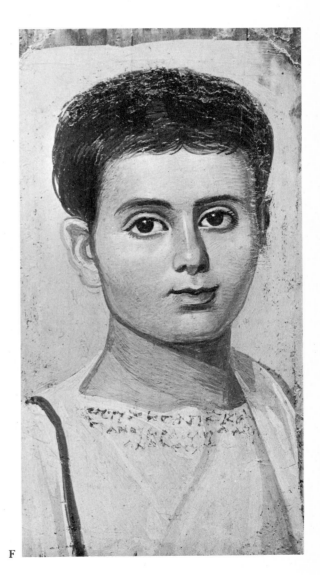

A. Vladimir, Cathedral of the Dormitian (1158–1161). 104' x 119' (*Drevnosti*, XVI, Mosk. Arkheolog. Obshch., 1900)
B. Moscow, Cathedral of the Annunciation (1484–1489). 79' x 125' x 138' high. (*Giraudon*)
C. Moscow, Cathedral of St. Basil (1555–1560). 130' x 124'. (*Giraudon*)
D. The Vision of Ezekiel, from Homilies of Gregory Nazianzus (880–886). Bib. Nat., Paris. (*Stoedtner*)
E. Vienna Genesis; Joseph's Dream. Nat. Lib., Vienna. (*Stoedtner*)
F. Portrait of a Boy, from the Faiyûm, Lower Egypt, Egyptian-Roman period (A.D. 2nd or 3rd century). MMA, Gift of Edward S. Harkness, 1918.

A.   Joshua Roll: Angels Appearing to Joshua before the Walls of Jericho (7th to 10th centuries). Vatican Lib. *(Stoedtner)*
B.   The Transfiguration. Sant' Apollinare in Classe, Ravenna. *(Stoedtner)*
C.   Christ and Saints (6th century). SS. Cosma e Damiano, Rome. *(Stoedtner)*
D.   The Sacrifice of Abraham (532–547). San Vitale, Ravenna. *(Stoedtner)*
E.   Emperor Justinian and His Attendants (526–547), mosaic. San Vitale, Ravenna. *(Alinari)*

A.   Emperor Justinian and Attendants (526–547), detail. San Vitale, Ravenna. *(Alinari)*
B.   The Empress Theodora and Her Attendants (before 547). San Vitale, Ravenna. *(Alinari)*
C.   The Empress Theodora and Her Attendants, detail. *(Alinari)*

A

B

C

D

E

F

A.   Throne of Maximianus (6th century). 47″ high. Archiepiscopal Palace, Ravenna. *(Omniafoto, Torino)*
B.   Ivory Diptych, Roman, right leaf. Victoria and Albert Mus., London.
C.   Sarcophagus of Theodore (6th to 7th centuries). 39½″ x 81″. Sant' Apollinare in Classe, Ravenna. *(Stoedtner)*
D.   Cordova, Mosque, arcades (8th–10th centuries). 38′ high. *(SNTO)*
E.   Cordova, Mosque, mihrab. *(Stoedtner)*
F.   Cordova, Mosque, dome. *(Stoedtner)*

A. Granada, The Alhambra, Court of the Myrtles (1368). 120′ x 75′. (SNTO)
B. Granada, The Alhambra, Court of the Lions (1377). 92′ x 52′.
C. Granada, The Alhambra, Hall of the Two Sisters (1377). c. 26′ x 26′. (Alinari)
D. Jerusalem, Dome of the Rock (691–1022). 98′ high. (Aramco)
E. Mschatta, detail of frieze (743–744). Staatliches Mus., Berlin. (Stoedtner)
F. Isfahan, Congregational Mosque, interior of north dome (1088). (E. Schroeder)
G. Isfahan, Congregational Mosque, northwest Iwan (12th century). (M. B. Smith)

A

B

C

D

E

A.   Physicians Cutting Plant, from a Dioscorides manuscript (1224). 5″ x 7″. Freer Gallery of Art, Wash., D.C.
B.   Stag and Doe, from a natural history manuscript (1297). 7½″ x 6¼″. Morgan Lib., N.Y.
C.   David Summoned to Be King, from a history of the world manuscript (1307). University Lib., Edinburgh.
D.   *Bihzad* (15th–16th centuries). Sultan Hussein Mirza Reveling, from a Bustan manuscript (1488). 12″ x 8½″. Royal Egyptian Lib., Cairo. (*Iran. Inst.*)
E.   *Bihzad*. King Darius and Herdsman, from a Bustan manuscript (1488). 12″ x 8½″. Royal Egyptian Lib. (*Iran. Inst.*)

A

D

B

C

E

A.   Meshed, Shrine of Imam Rida, the Old Court (15th century) and Minaret (*c.* 1730). (*Iran. Inst.*)
B.   Jahangir (*c.* 1615). 1½″ x 1½″. MFA.
C.   Agra, Pearl Mosque (1646–1653). Court, 150′ x 150′. (*Avery Lib., Columbia U.*)
D.   Illumination, from Hamza-namah (16th century). 27″ x 21″. MMA, Rogers Fund, 1918.
E.   Agra, Taj Mahal (17th century). 186′ x 186′ x 187′ high. *(Govt. of India)*

[1] For pre-Islamic Persia, see Pl. 12-13. For other Indian art, see Pl. 305-308.

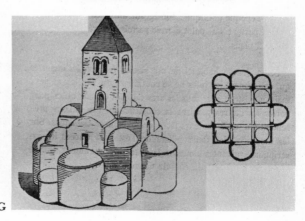

A.   Aachen, Charlemagne's Chapel, interior (796–804). Diameter, 48′. *(Marburg)*
B.   Brixworth, Church, interior (*c.* 670). Nave, 30′ wide.
C.   Earl's Barton, Church (10th century). *c.* 40′ wide. *(Stoedtner)*
D.   Oviedo (near), Santa Maria de Naranco, interior (9th century). 16′ 6″ wide.
E.   Lorsch, Gatehouse (880). 33′ high. *(Marburg)*
F.   León, San Isidoro, Panteón de los Reyes (1005). *c.* 25′ x 25′. *(SNTO)*
G.   Germigny-des-Prés, reconstruction (806). 58′ x 58′. *(Stoedtner)*

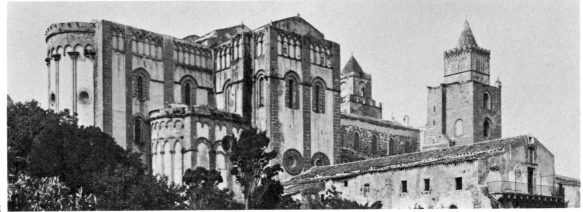

A.   Palermo, Cappella Palatina (1132). 108' x 42'. *(Alinari)*
B.   Cefalù, Cathedral, façade (begun 1145). 95' wide. *(Alinari)*
C.   Cefalù, Cathedral, apse and flank. 243' long. *(Alinari)*
D.   Monreale, Cathedral, interior (1174–1189). 334' x 131'. *(Alinari)*
E.   Monreale, Cathedral, cloister.

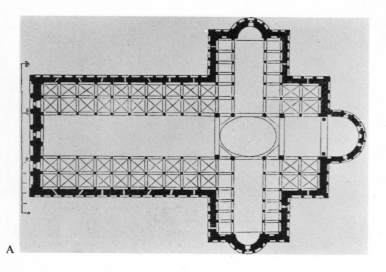

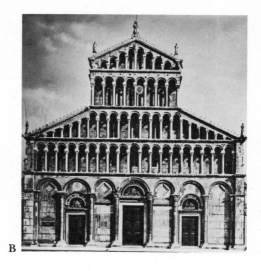

A.   Pisa, Cathedral (1063–1092). 320′ x 230′. *(Stoedtner)*
B.   Pisa, Cathedral, façade. 115′ wide. *(Stoedtner)*
C.   Pisa, Cathedral, campanile. *(Stoedtner)*
D.   Pisa, Cathedral, interior. *(Stoedtner)*
E.   Florence, San Miniato, façade (begun 1013). 80′ wide. *(Alinari)*
F.   Florence, San Miniato, interior. Nave, 30′ wide. *(Stoedtner)*

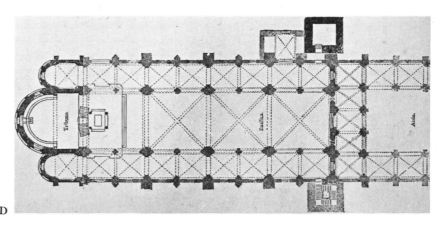

A.   Lucca, Cathedral (1060–1204). Façade, 84′ wide.
B.   Florence, Baptistry, interior (*c.* 1100).
C.   Florence, Baptistry, section. Diameter, 90′.
D.   Milan, Sant' Ambrogio (1046–1196). Length, including atrium, 390′; 92′ wide. *(Stoedtner)*
E.   Milan, Sant' Ambrogio, longitudinal section of one bay. *(Stoedtner)*
F.   Milan, Sant' Ambrogio, nave. *(Stoedtner)*

A.   Milan, Sant' Ambrogio (1064–1196). Total length, 390'. *(Stoedtner)*
B.   Pavia, San Michele, façade (12th century). 95' wide. *(Alinari)*
C.   Worms, Cathedral (1171–1192). 438' long. *(Marburg)*
D.   Bamberg, Cathedral (13th century). 312' x 94' x 84' high. *(Stoedtner)*
E.   Mainz, Cathedral, interior (12th–13th centuries). 90' high. *(Germ. Tour Inf.)*
F.   Hildesheim, St. Michael's, interior (1186). Nave, 29' wide x 58' high. *(Germ. Tour Inf.)*

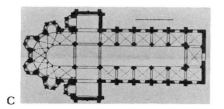

A.   Arles, St. Trophîme, porch (*c.* 1150). *c.* 40′ wide. *(Stoedtner)*
B.   Saint-Gilles, porch (12th century). 75′ wide. *(Stoedtner)*
C.   Clermont-Ferrand, Notre Dame du Port (11th century). 164′ x 85′. *(Stoedtner)*
D.   Clermont-Ferrand, Notre Dame du Port, transverse section through nave. 52½″ wide. *(Stoedtner)*
E.   Clermont-Ferrand, Notre Dame du Port, east end. *(Stoedtner)*
F.   Clermont-Ferrand, Notre Dame du Port, interior.

A

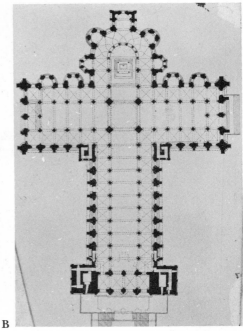

B

D

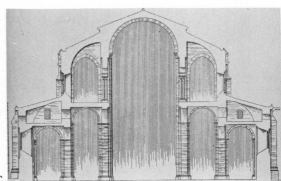

C

E

A.   Toro, La Colegiata (late 12th century). *(SNTO)*
B.   Santiago de Compostela (1075–1128). 308′ x 207′.
C. Toulouse, St. Sernin, transverse section through nave (1080–1096). 110′ wide. *(Stoedtner)*
D.   Santiago de Compostela, nave. 164′ x 33′ x 69′ high.
E.   Toulouse, St. Sernin, east end. Total height, 215′. *(Stoedtner)*

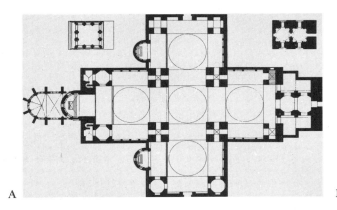

A

B

C

D

E

A. Périgueux, St. Front (11th century). Main church, 185′ x 185′. *(Stoedtner)*
B. Périgueux, St. Front. Tower, 215′ high. *(Stoedtner)*
C. Périgueux, St. Front. Domes, 90′ high. *(Stoedtner)*
D. Angoulême, Cathedral (1105–1128). 50′ wide; domes, 68′ high. *(Stoedtner)*
E. Poitiers, Notre Dame la Grande (11th century). 58′ wide x 59′ high. *(French Embassy)*

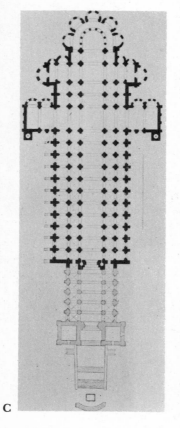

A.   Cluny, Abbey, restored (1088–1130). *(Stoedtner)*
B.   Cluny, Abbey, interior.
C.   Cluny, Abbey. 589′ x 74′. *(Stoedtner)*
D.   Tournus, St. Philibert, longitudinal section (1009–1019). Nave, 89′ long. *(Stoedtner)*
E.   Vézelay, La Madeleine, nave (11th century). 33′ wide. *(French Embassy)*.

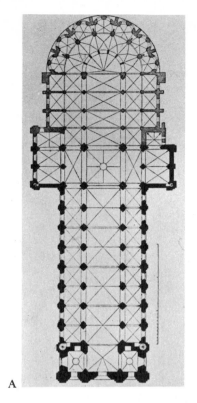

A.   Caen, St. Étienne (1064–1077). 360′ x 73′. *(Stoedtner)*
B.   Caen, St. Étienne, façade. 295′ high. *(Stoedtner)*
C.   Caen, St. Étienne, longitudinal section of one bay. Vaults, *c.* 1135. *(Stoedtner)*
D.   Caen, St. Étienne, nave. 32′ wide. *(Stoedtner)*

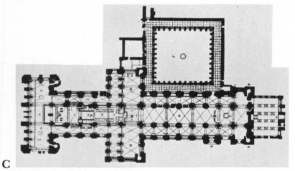

A.   Caen, La Trinité (1062). 79′ wide. *(FGTO)*
B.   Caen, La Trinité, nave. 28′ wide. *(FGTO)*
C.   Durham, Cathedral (1096–1133). Total length, 469′.
D.   Durham Cathedral.
E.   Durham, Cathedral, nave. 39′ wide x 72′ high.

A

B

C

D

E

F

A.　Winchester, Cathedral, transept (1079–1093). 80′ wide, including aisles.
B.　Utrecht Psalter (early 9th century). Battle scene. Univ. Lib., Utrecht. *(Stoedtner)*
C.　Iffley, Church (12th century). *(Stoedtner)*
D.　Bayeux Embroidery (11th century). 1′ 8½″ high. Arrival of the Normans at Pevensey. Mus. Reine Mathilde, Bayeux. *(Stoedtner)*
E.　Ely, Cathedral, nave (12th century). Nave, 208′ long x 62′ high.
F.　Bayeux Embroidery (11th century). 1′ 8½″ high. Scene from Battle of Hastings. Mus. Reine Mathilde, Bayeux. *(Pub. Lib., Bayeux)*

A

B

C

D

E

F

A.   Book of Durrow (7th century). Trinity College, Dublin. *(Stoedtner)*
B.   Book of Kells (8th century). Initial page-XPI. Trinity College, Dublin. *(Stoedtner)*
C.   Book of Lindisfarne (8th century). Cross page. Brit. Mus. *(Stoedtner)*
D.   British Gospel Book (8th century). Cross St. Gall, Switzerland. *(Stoedtner)*
E.   Gospel Otto III (*c*. 1000). Transfiguration. Bayer. Staatsbib, Munich
F.   Irish Gospel Book (8th century). St. Mark. St. Gall, Switzerland. *(Stoedtner)*

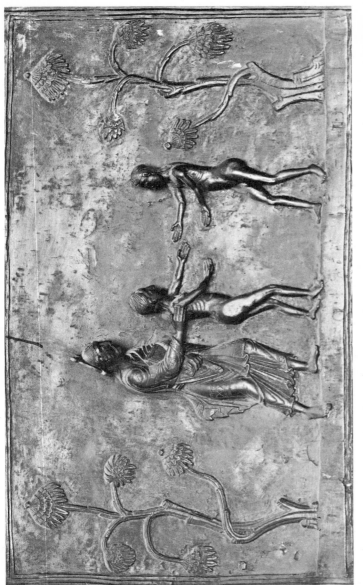

A. Cross from Monasterboice, county in South Ireland. (*Mansell*)
B. The Creation of Eve (1007–1015), relief. St. Bernard's door, Cathedral, Hildesheim. (*Marburg*)
C. Arles, St. Trophime (12th century), west portal. (*Stoedtner*)
D. Column: Jesus and the Samaritan (11th century). Cathedral, Hildesheim. (*Stoedtner*)

A. Tympanum: Christ Sending Forth the Apostles (*c.* 1130). 31′ 4″ wide. La Madeleine, Vézelay. *(Stoedtner)*
B. Tympanum: Last Judgment (early 12th century). West portal, St. Lazare, Autun. *(Stoedtner)*
C. Tympanum (12th century). 18′ 8″ wide. St. Pierre, Moissac. *(Stoedtner)*
D. Tympanum: Christ in Mastery, with Symbols of Evangelists (1145–1155). Royal Portal, west, Cathedral, Chartres. *(Stoedtner)*

A

B

C

D

A.   Prophet Isaiah. West portal, Church, Souillac. *(Stoedtner)*
B.   Virgin and Child (School of Auvergne, late 12th century).   31″ high, 12¾″ wide. MMA, Gift of J. Pierpont Morgan, 1916.
C.   Virgin and Child (early 15th century). 16½″ high. MMA, Bequest of George Blumenthal, 1941.
D.   Virgin and Child—Notre Dame de Grasse (15th century). Mus. des Augustins, Toulouse.

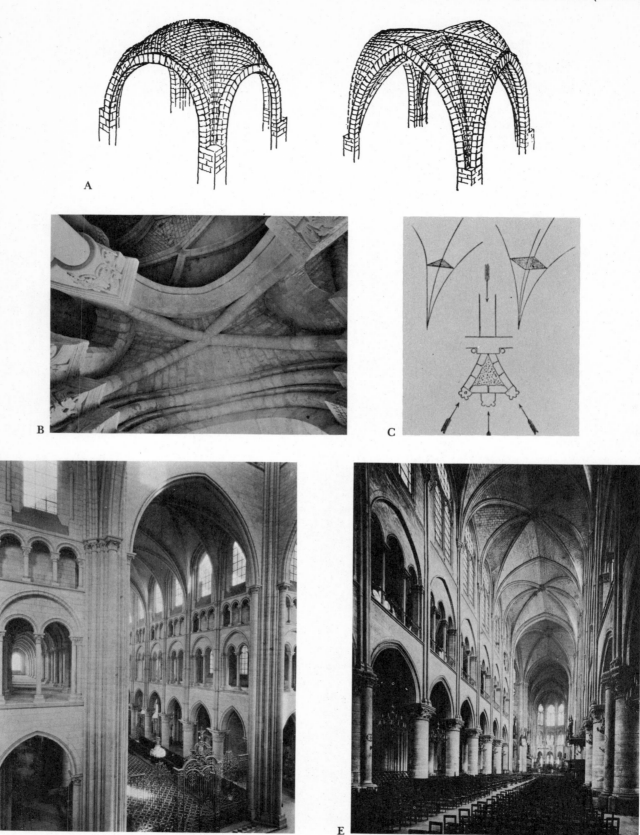

A.   Romanesque and Gothic vaults. (Kimball and Edgell, *Hist. of Arch.*, Harper)
B.   Morienval, Church, ambulatory vault (*c.* 1120).
C.   Stilting. (C. H. Moore, *The Medieval Church Architecture of England*, The Macmillan Company)
D.   Laon, Cathedral, nave (12th century). Nave and aisles, 67′ wide; vaults, 78′ high.
E.   Paris, Notre Dame (1163–1235). Nave, 46′ wide; vaults, 110′ high. *(Stoedtner)*

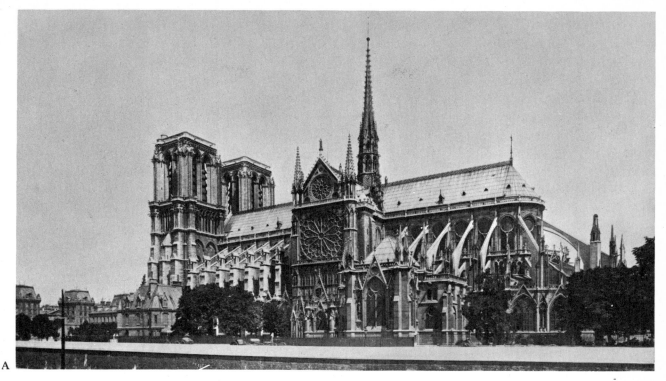

A

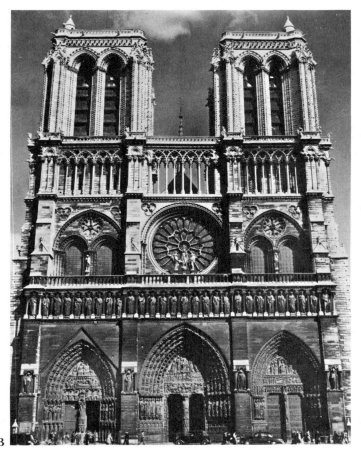

B

C

D

E

A.   Paris, Notre Dame, flank. 417′ long.
B.   Paris, Notre Dame, façade. 135′ wide; towers, 207′ high. *(FGTO)*
C.   Paris, Sainte Chapelle (1245–1248). Interior length 98′; 35′ wide.
D.   Senlis, Cathedral, spire (1155–1191). Total height, 250′. *(FGTO)*
E.   Bourges, Cathedral, nave (13th century). 120′ high. *(Stoedtner)*

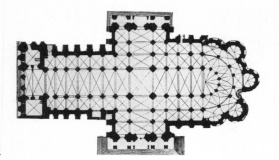

A

C

B

D

E

A.   Chartres, Cathedral (1194–1260). 427′ long. (A. de Baudot and A. Perrault-Dabot, *Les Cathédrales de France*)
B.   Chartres, Cathedral, facade. 157′ wide; north spire, 377′ high; south spire, 344′ high. *(FGTO)*
C.   Chartres, Cathedral, transverse section. (Baudot and Perrault-Dabot)
D.   Chartres, Cathedral, from air. *(Aero Photo)*
E.   Chartres, Cathedral, nave. 54′ wide; vaults, 121′ high.

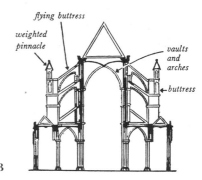

A. Amiens, Cathedral (1220–1279). Interior length, 438'; nave width, 48'; vaults, 139' high.
B. Amiens, Cathedral, transverse section.
C. Amiens, Cathedral, triforium and clearstory of the nave. *(Clarence Ward)*
D. Amiens, Cathedral, vaults. *(Clarence Ward)*
E. Reims, Cathedral (1211–1290). Towers, 267' high. *(FGTO)*
F. Reims, Cathedral, flank. 453' long.

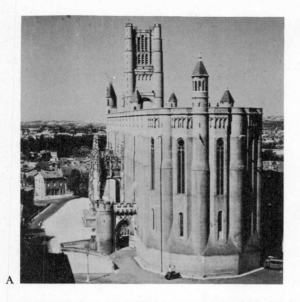

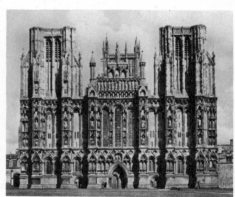

A.   Albi, Cathedral (1282–1390). Walls, 130' high. *(French Embassy)*
B.   Rouen, Tour de Beurre (1509–1530). 252' high. *(FGTO)*
C.   Rouen, St. Maclou, façade (1432–1511). 75' wide. *(Stoedtner)*
D.   Canterbury, Cathedral, choir (1174–1180). 180' long; 71' high. *(BIS)*
E.   Wells, Cathedral, façade (1206–1242). 147' wide.
F.   Wells, Cathedral, nave (1174–1191). 67' high. *(BIS)*

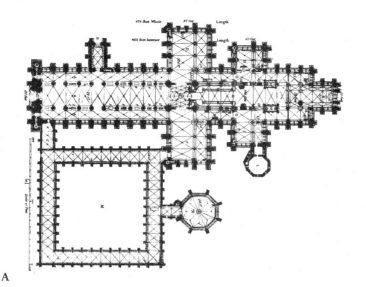

A. Salisbury, Cathedral (1220–1258). 473′ x 230′. *(Stoedtner)*
B. Salisbury, Cathedral, from northeast. Spire, 404′ high.
C. Salisbury, Cathedral, nave. 40′ wide; vaults, 81′ high. *(Stoedtner)*
D. Lincoln, Cathedral, Angel Choir (1255–1280). Nave and aisles, *c.* 88′ wide. *(Stoedtner)*
E. Exeter, Cathedral, nave (1280–1370). 66′ high. *(BIS)*
F. Melrose Abbey (14th–15th centuries). Transept, 42′ 6″ wide. *(Stoedtner)*

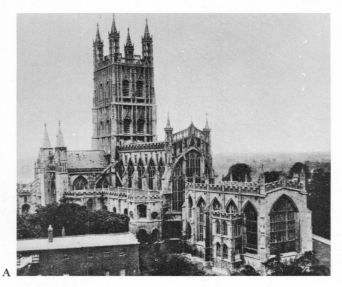

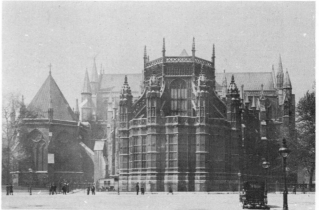

A.   Gloucester, Cathedral (14th–15th centuries). Length east of tower, 180′; tower, 225′ high. *(Stoedtner)*
B.   Gloucester, Cathedral, choir (1351). East window, 72′ x 38′; vaults, 86′ high.
C.   Gloucester, Cathedral, cloister (1351–1412). 147′ long x 12′ wide x 18′ 6″ high. *(Stoedtner)*
D.   London, Westminster Abbey, Henry VII's Chapel (1502–1520). *c.* 75′ wide. *(Stoedtner)*
E.   London, Westminster Abbey, Henry VII's Chapel, vaults. *(Stoedtner)*

A. Ulm, Cathedral (1377–1529). Tower, 528′ high. *(Stoedtner)*
B. Marburg, St. Elizabeth (1235–1283). 67′ 3″ high. *(Marburg)*
C. San Galgano, Abbey Church (1240–1268). *(Alinari)*
D. Florence, Cathedral (begun 1294). 556′ long. *(Stoedtner)*
E. Orvieto. Cathedral, façade (1290–1309).
F. Orvieto, Cathedral, nave. 343′ x 108′.

A.   Milan, Cathedral (begun 1386). Façade, 219′ wide. *(Ist. Ital. Cult.)*
B.   Milan, Cathedral, nave. 54′ wide x 157′ high. *(Stoedtner)*
C.   Burgos, Cathedral, interior (begun 1221). 300′ long; nave and aisles, 82′ wide. *(SNTO)*
D.   Burgos, Cathedral. Towers (1442–1458). 275′ high. *(Stoedtner)*
E.   Batalha, Santa Maria da Victoria (15th century). *(Helga Schmidt-Glassner, Stuttgart)*

A.   Carcassonne (13th century).
B.   Bodiam Castle (1386). 175′ x 178′; towers, 60′ 4″ high. *(BIS)*
C.   Ypres, Cloth Hall (1200–1304). 440′ long.
D.   Hildesheim, Butchers' Guild Hall (1529).
E.   Valencia, La Lonja (1482). 118′ x 70′. *(Stoedtner)*

A

B

C

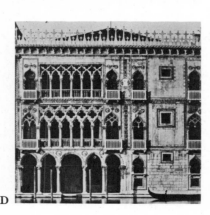

D

E

A.   Compton Wynyates (*c.* 1520). Façade, *c.* 120′ long. *(BIS)*
B.   Bourges, Jacques Coeur House (1443). Façade, *c.* 150′ long. *(Stoedtner)*
C.   Siena, Palazzo Pubblico (1289–1309). 190′ wide. *(Stoedtner)*
D.   Venice, Ca d'Oro (15th century). 69′ wide. *(Stoedtner)*
E.   Venice, Ducal Palace (1424–1442). *c.* 260′ long. *(Alinari)*

A

B

C

D

E

A.   St. Matthew. Notre Dame de la Couture, Le Mans. *(Stoedtner)*
B.   *Villard de Honnecourt.* Sketchbook (*c.* 1240). Plate **XXXVI**. Biblio. Nat., Paris. *(Arch. Photo.)*
C.   Tympanum, detail. Cathedral, Bourges. *(Stoedtner)*
D.   The Smiling Angel. Cathedral, Reims. *(Bulloz)*
E.   Annunciation and Visitation (*c.* 1225–1235). 10′ 2″ high. West façade, Cathedral, Reims. *(French Embassy)*

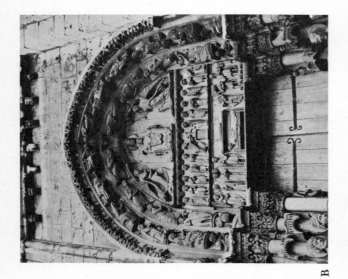

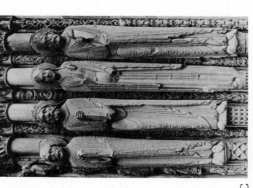

A.   North Portal (c. 1145–1170). Cathedral, Chartres. (French Cult. Serv.)
B.   Western, or Royal, Portal (c. 1145–1170). 20' 6" high. Cathedral, Chartres. (French Embassy)
C.   King's Portal (c. 1145–1170). Statues on the right side, Cathedral, Chartres. (Stoedtner)
D.   January, February, October, November (c. 1145–1170). Cathedral, Chartres. (Stoedtner)
E.   Head of Jesse and Angel (c. 1145–1170). Cathedral, Chartres. (Stoedtner)
F.   Annunciation (12th century). West central window, Cathedral Chartres. c. 41⅜" x 40⅛". (James R. Johnson, Cleveland Mus. Art)

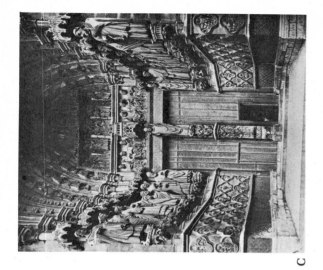

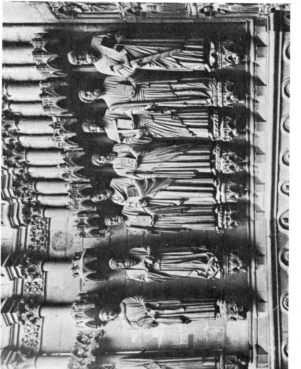

A. Christ (Le Beau Dieu), detail of central portal, west façade (c. 1220–1230). 10' high. Cathedral, Amiens. (*French Embassy*)
B. Central portal, west façade, with Le Beau Dieu. 24' 6", height of trumeau. Cathedral, Amiens.
C. St. Firmin (1220–1248). Cathedral, Amiens. (*Stoedtner*)
D. Vierge Dorée, south transept portal (c. 1250). 10' high. Cathedral, Amiens. (*Stoedtner*)
E. Portal of Christ: Apostles and Prophets (1220–1248). Cathedral, Amiens. (*Stoedtner*)
F. *Giovanni Pisano* (c. 1250–1330). Madonna and Child. Cathedral, Pisa. (*Stoedtner*)

A.   Seducer and Foolish Virgins. Cathedral, Strasbourg. *(Stoedtner)*
B.   Annunciation (13th century). Cathedral, Bamberg. *(Stoedtner)*
C.   *Andrea Pisano* (*c.* 1270–1349). Visitation (1330–1339). Baptistry, Florence. *(Stoedtner)*
D.   Equestrian Figure of a Knight (*c.* 1230–1240). Cathedral, Bamberg. *(GTIO)*
E.   Margrave Ekkehard II and Uta (*c.* 1250–1260). Cathedral, Naumburg. *(Stoedtner)*

A.   *Claus Sluter* (*fl. c.* 1380; *d.* 1406). Madonna (1395–1403). Left portal, Chartreuse de Champmol, Dijon. (*Stoedtner*)
B.   *Claus Sluter*. Madonna (1395–1403). Right portal, Chartreuse de Champmol. (*Stoedtner*)
C.   *Claus Sluter*. Well of Moses. Daniel and Isaiah (1395–1406). 5′ 8″ high. Chartreuse de Champmol. (*Stoedtner*)
D.   *Claus Sluter*. Well of Moses: Jeremiah, Moses, David. (*Stoedtner*)
E.   *Giovanni Cimabue* (*c.* 1240–1301). Madonna Enthroned with Saints and Angels (1270–1285). 12′ 6″ x 7′ 4″. Uffizi. (*Alinari*)
F.   *Giovanni Cimabue*. Portrait of St. Francis. Lower Church, Assisi. (*Alinari*)
G.   *Bonaventura Berlinghieri*. St. Francis Receiving the Stigmata. 32″ x 20″. Uffizi. (*Alinari*)

A.   *Giotto di Bondone* (*c.* 1266–1336). Miracle of the Spring (*c.* 1296–1300). Upper Church, Assisi. *(Alinari)*
B.   *Giotto di Bondone.* The Betrayal (1303–1306). Arena Chapel, Padua. *(Stoedtner)*
C.   *Giotto di Bondone.* The Bewailing of Christ (1303–1306). 7′ 7″ x 7′ 9″. Arena Chapel, Padua. *(Stoedtner)*
D.   *Giotto di Bondone.* Death of St. Francis (1303–1306). Bardi Chapel, Sante Croce, Florence.
E.   *Giotto di Bondone,* Meeting of Joachim and Anna (1303–1306). 7′ 7⁵⁄₁₆″ x 8′ 3³⁄₁₆″. Arena Chapel, Padua. *(Stoedtner)*
F.   *Taddeo Gaddi* (*d.* 1366). Joachim and Anna at the Golden Gate. Santa Croce, Florence. *(Stoedtner)*

A. *Francesco Traini* (?). Triumph of Death (*c.* 1350). Campo Santo, Pisa. Partially destroyed, 1944. *(Stoedtner)*
B. *Duccio di Buoninsegna* (*c.* 1255/60–1318/19). Crucifixion. Opera del Duomo, Siena. *(Stoedtner)*
C. *Ambrogio Lorenzetti* (*fl.* 1319–1347). Allegory of Good Government (1337–1343). Palazzo Pubblico, Siena. *(Stoedtner)*
D. *Duccio di Buoninsegna.* Christ at the Mt. of Olives, and Betrayal. Opera del Duomo, Siena. *(Stoedtner)*
E. *Ambrogio Lorenzetti.* Deposition. San Francisco, Assisi. *(Stoedtner)*
F. *Simone Martini* (*c.* 1283–1344). Sant' Ansano Annunciation (1333). 9′ 10″ x 8′ 7″. Uffizi. *(Stoedtner)*

A.   *Maso di Banco* or *Giottino*. A Miracle of St. Sylvester (*c.* 1340), fresco. *c.* 8′ 11″ x 14′ 6¾″. Santa Croce, Florence. *(Alinari)*
B.   Portrait of Jean le Bon, King of France (1360). 26″ x 17¼″. Louvre. *(Arch. Photo.)*
C.   *Simone Martini* (*c.* 1283–1344). Fogliano da Reggio (1323). Pal. Pub., Siena.
D.   "Wilton Diptych": Richard II with Three Saints before the Madonna (*c.* 1415). Each panel, 18″ x 11½″.
Nat. Gal., London. *(Stoedtner)*

A

B

C

D

A. *Robert Campin* (1378/9–1444). The Merode Altarpiece (*c.* 1420–1430). Triptych: (1) *left,* Donors in Walled Garden; (2) *center,* Annunciation; (3) *right,* Joseph in His Carpenter Shop. 29⅜″ high; 58½″ wide. MMA, Cloisters Collection.

B. *Jan van Eyck* (*c.* 1385–1441). The Three Marys at the Tomb. Collection of Sir Herbert Cook, Richmond. *(Bruckmann)*

C. *Hubert van Eyck* (*c.* 1366–1426) and *Jan van Eyck*. Adoration of the Lamb, altarpiece (*c.* 1415–1432). 8′ wide. St. Bavon, Ghent. *(Stoedtner)*

D. *Hubert van Eyck* and *Jan van Eyck*. Singing Angels. 5′ 3″ x 2′ 3″. Panel, altarpiece, St. Bavon, Ghent.

A. *Jan van Eyck* (*c.* 1385–1441). Madonna of Chancellor Rolin (*c.* 1432). 26″ x 24½″. Louvre. *(Stoedtner)*
B. *Rogier van der Weyden* (*c.* 1399–1464). St. Luke Making a Portrait of the Virgin. 54½″ x 43¾″. MFA.
C. *Jan van Eyck*. St. Barbara. Antwerp. *(Stoedtner)*
D. *Jan van Eyck*. St. Francis Receiving the Stigmata (1438). 5″ x 5¾″. John C. Johnson Coll., Philadelphia.
E. *Rogier van der Weyden*. Portrait of a Lady. 14½″ x 10¾″. Nat. Gal., Wash., Mellon Coll.

A. *Jan van Eyck* (*c.* 1385–1441). Virgin and Child with Saints and a Donor. 19 1/16″ x 24 1/2″. Frick Mus., N. Y., 1954.
B. *Rogier van der Weyden* (*c.* 1399–1464). Deposition (1440). 7′ x 8′ 5″. Prado, Madrid.
C. *Hugo van der Goes* (*c.* 1440–1482). Portinari Altarpiece, central panel: Adoration of the Shepherds (1476). 8′ 1″ x 10″.
Uffizi. (*Alinari*)

A. *Hans Memling* (*c.* 1430–1494). Shrine of St. Ursula, Martyrdom of the Virgins (1489). Hospital of St. John, Bruges. *(Stoedtner)*
B.   *Dirk Bouts* (1415–1475). Martyrdom of St. Erasmus. St. Peter's, Louvain. *(Stoedtner)*
C.   *Quentin Massys* (1464/5–1530). Mourning of Christ. Roy. Mus. Fine Arts, Antwerp. *(Bruckmann)*
D.   *Dirk Bouts.* The Last Supper (*c.* 1465). Altar, central panel, 71″ x 59″. St. Peter's, Louvain. *(Stoedtner)*
E.   *Joos van Cleve the Elder* (1485–1540). The Crucifixion. 31½″ x 25″. MFA.
F.   *Gerard David* (*d.* 1523). Baptism of Christ. Bruges. *(Stoedtner)*

A.   *Upper Rhine Master*. Garden of Paradise (1410). Staedel. *(Stoedtner)*
B.   *Martin Schongauer* (1453–1491). The Virgin in the Courtyard. MFA, Purchase, Dick Fund, 1940.
C.   *Stephan Lochner* (d. 1451). Adoration of the Magi. Altarpiece, central panel, Cathedral, Cologne. *(Stoedtner)*
D.   *Conrad Witz* (1400/10–1444/6). Miraculous Draft of Fishes (1444). 51″ x 61″. Mus. d'Art et d'Hist., Geneva. *(Stoedtner)*
E.   *Martin Schongauer*. Madonna in Rose Garden (1473). Colmar. *(Stoedtner)*

A

B

C

D

A.   *German School* (15th century). St. Dorothy, a woodcut. Staat. Graph. Samm., Munich. *(Stoedtner)*
B.   *German School*. St. Christopher Bearing the Infant Christ (1423), a woodcut. John Rylands Lib., Manchester. *(Stoedtner)*
C.   *Veit Stoss* (1440?–1533). Altar of the Virgin. Cracow. *(Stoedtner)*
D.   *Albrecht Dürer* (1471–1528). Apocalypse—Four Horsemen (1498). *(Stoedtner)*

A

B

C

D

A.   *Martin Schongauer* (1453–1491). Crozier, engraving. MMA, Purchase, Dick Fund, 1940.
B.   *Albrecht Dürer* (1471–1528). The Knight, Death, and the Devil. MMA, Dick Fund, 1943.
C.   *Albrecht Dürer.* Apocalypse—Saint Michael Slaying the Dragon (1498). MMA, Gift of Junius S. Morgan, 1919.
D.   *Albrecht Dürer.* The Last Supper, woodcut. Nat. Gal., Wash., Gift of W. G. Russell Allen.

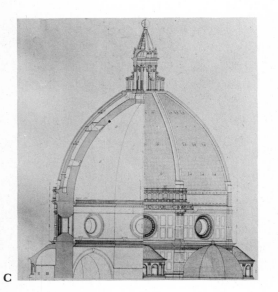

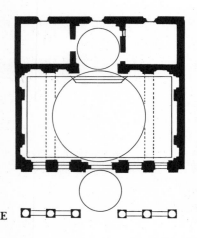

A.   *Brunelleschi* (1377–1446). Florence, Foundlings Hospital (1421). 180′ wide. *(Stoedtner)*
B.   *Brunelleschi.* Florence, Cathedral, dome (1418–1434). Total height, 367′. *(Stoedtner)*
C.   Florence, Cathedral, dome section. Diameter, *c.* 140′. *(Stoedtner)*
D.   *Brunelleschi.* Florence. San Lorenzo (1425). Nave. 250′ long x 95′ wide x 69′ 6″ high. *(Stoedtner)*
E.   *Brunelleschi.* Florence, Pazzi Chapel (*c.* 1429). Interior 59′ 9″ x 35′ 8″. EMU.
F.   Florence, Pazzi Chapel, section. *(Stoedtner)*
G.   Florence, Pazzi Chapel, interior. *(Stoedtner)*

A. *Brunelleschi* (1377–1446). Florence, Pazzi Chapel. Main cornice, 40' high.
B. *Michelozzo* (1396–1472). Florence, Riccardi Palace (1444–1459), plan. 225' x 190'. EMU.
C.   Florence, Riccardi Palace, court. *(Stoedtner)*
D.   Florence, Riccardi Palace. 80' high.
E. *Alberti* (1404–1472). Florence, Rucellai Palace (1451–1455). 69' high. *(Stoedtner)*

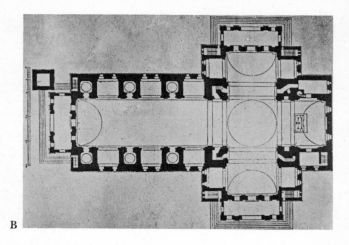

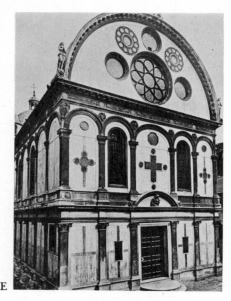

A.   *Alberti* (1404–1472). Rimini, San Francesco (1447–1455). Façade, 97′ wide. *(Stoedtner)*
B.   *Alberti*. Mantua, Sant' Andrea (begun *c.* 1470). 300′ x 171′. *(Stoedtner)*
C.   Mantua, Sant' Andrea. *(Stoedtner)*
D.   Mantua, Sant' Andrea, interior. *(Alinari)*
E. *P. Lombardo* (*c.* 1435–1515). Venice, Santa Maria dei Miracoli (1481–1499). 53′ 6″ high. *(Stoedtner)*
F.   Venice, Santa Maria dei Miracoli, interior. 32′ 7″ wide. *(Stoedtner)*

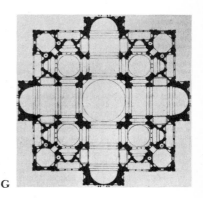

A. *Fra Giocondo* (*c.* 1433–1515). Verona, Palazzo del Consiglio (1476). 116′ wide x 56′ high. *(Alinari)*
B. *Amadeo* and others. Pavia, Certosa, façade (late 15th century). 125′ wide, 100′ high in center. *(Ist. Ital. Cult.)*
C. *P. Lombardo* (*c.* 1435–1515). Venice, Palazzo Vendramin (1481–1509). 79′ high. *(Alinari)*
D. *Bramante* (1444–1514). Milan, Santa Maria delle Grazie (1492–1499). 102′ wide across transepts. *(Stoedtner)*
E. *Bramante?* Rome, Palazzo Cancelleria (1486–1496). Façade, 295′ x 80′. *(Stoedtner)*
F. *Bramante.* Rome, San Pietro in Montorio, Tempietto (1502). Diameter of colonnade, 29′; total height, 46′. *(Stoedtner)*
G. *Bramante.* Rome, St. Peter's (1506–1514). *c.* 560′ x 560′. *(Stoedtner)*

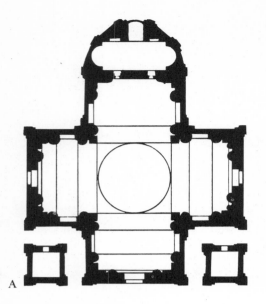

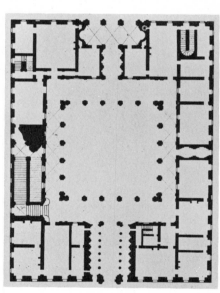

A. *Antonio da Sangallo the Elder (1455–1534)*. Montepulciano San Biagio (*c.* 1518–1537), plan. *c.* 120′ x 120′. EMU.
B.   Montepulciano, San Biagio. *(Alinari)*
C.   Montepulciano, San Biagio, interior. *(Stoedtner)*
D. *Antonio da Sangallo the Younger (1485–1546)*. Rome, Farnese Palace (1534). 185′ x 235′. *(Stoedtner)*
E.   Rome, Farnese Palace, façade. 185′ x 96′ 6″. *(Stoedtner)*
F. *Antonio da Sangallo the Younger* and *Michelangelo (1475–1564)*. Rome, Farnese Palace, court. 81′ x 81′. *(Stoedtner)*

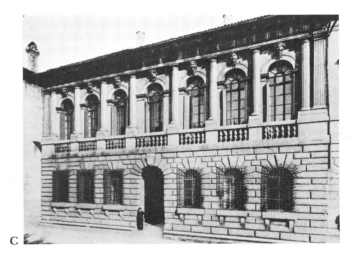

A. *Peruzzi* (1481–1536). Rome, Palazzo Massimi (1535). 64′ 7″ high. *(Stoedtner)*
B. *Peruzzi.* Rome, Villa Farnesina (1509–1511). *(Stoedtner)*
C. *Sanmicheli* (1484–1559). Verona, Palazzo Pompei (c. 1530). 70′ 3″ wide x 44′ high. *(Stoedtner)*
D. *Sanmicheli.* Verona, Palazzo Bevilacqua (1527). 77′ wide x 53′ high. *(Stoedtner)*
E. *Sansovino* (1486–1570). Venice, Library (1536). 275′ long x 58′ high. *(Stoedtner)*

A.   *Jacopo della Quercia* (*c.* 1374–1438). Baptismal Font. San Giovanni, Siena. *(Alinari)*
B.   *Jacopo della Quercia.* Madonna. Piazza del Campo, Siena. *(Stoedtner)*
C.   *Filippo Brunelleschi* (1377–1446). Sacrifice of Isaac. Nat. Mus., Florence. *(Alinari)*
D. *Jacopo della Quercia.* The Creation of Adam (1425–1438). 34½″ x 27½″. San Petronio, Bologna. *(Stoedtner)*
E.   *Lorenzo Ghiberti* (*c.* 1378–1455). Sacrifice of Isaac (1401–1402). 21″ x 17½″. Nat. Mus., Florence. *(Stoedtner)*

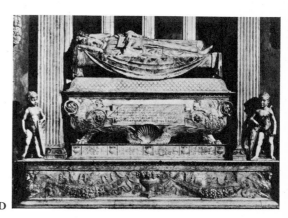

A. *Lorenzo Ghiberti* (*c.* 1378–1455). Detail of enframing (see B.). "Gates of Paradise" (*c.* 1435).
Baptistery, Florence. *(Stoedtner)*

B. *Lorenzo Ghiberti.* Creation of Man (*c.* 1435). 31¼" wide. "Gates of Paradise," Baptistery, Florence. *(Stoedtner)*

C. *Antonio Rossellino* (1427?–1479). Tomb of Cardinal of Portugal. *c.* 92½" long. San Miniato, Florence. *(Stoedtner)*

D. *Desiderio da Settignano* (*c.* 1428–1464). Tomb of Carlo Marsuppini (*c.* 1455). *c.* 91" long. Santa Croce, Florence. *(Stoedtner)*

E. *Nanni di Banco* (1374?–1420). St. Luke. *c.* 80" high. Statue formerly in Cathedral, Florence. *(Stoedtner)*

F. *Donatello* (*c.* 1386–1466). Mary Magdalen (1454–1455), 74" high. San Giovanni, Florence. *(Stoedtner)*

A.   *Donatello* (*c.* 1386–1466). Equestrian Monument of Gattamelata (1445–1450). 11′ x 13′. Piazza San Antonio, Padua. *(Alinari)*

B.   *Donatello.* St. George Tabernacle (1416). 82″ high. Nat. Mus., Florence. *(Alinari)*

C.   *Andrea del Verrocchio* (*c.* 1435–1488). Equestrian monument of Bartolommeo Colleoni (1485–1488). 13′ high. Campo SS. Giovanni e Paolo, Venice. *(ITIO)*

D.   *Donatello.* David (*c.* 1430–1432). 62¼″ high. Nat. Mus., Florence. *(Stoedtner)*

E.   *Andrea del Verrocchio.* David. *c.* 47¼″ high. Bargello, Florence. *(Stoedtner)*

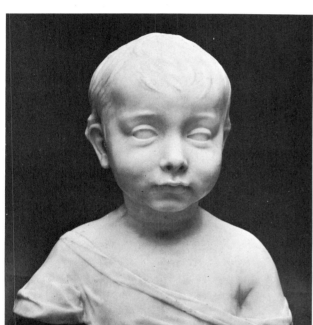

A. *Luca della Robbia* (1400–1482). Singing Gallery, or Cantoria (1431–1438). *c.* 18′ 6″ over-all length. Mus., Cathedral, Florence. *(Stoedtner)*

B. *Donatello* (*c.* 1386–1466). Singing Gallery (1433–1438). 10′ 17″ x 18′ 8″. Mus., Cathedral, Florence. *(Stoedtner)*

C. *Desiderio da Settignano* (*c.* 1428–1464). Bust of a Little Boy. 10-11/32″ x 9¾″ x 5⅞″. Nat. Gal., Wash.

D. *Donatello* (?). Niccolo da Uzzano (*c.* 1432). *c.* 18½″ high. Nat. Mus., Florence. *(Stoedtner)*

E. *Andrea del Verrocchio* (*c.* 1435–1488). Putto with Dolphin (*c.* 1470). 27″ without base. Palazzo Vecchio, Florence. *(Stoedtner)*

F. *Antonio Pollaiuolo* (1432–1498). Hercules and Antaeus (*c.* 1475). 18″ high. Nat. Mus., Florence. *(Alinari)*

A.   *Fra Angelico* (1387–1455). Coronation of the Virgin (*c.* 1430). San Marco, Florence. *(Stoedtner)*
B.   *Fra Angelico.* The Annunciation (*c.* 1445–1450). 7'6" x 10'5". San Marco, Florence. *(Stoedtner)*
C.   *Domenico Veneziano* (1400–1461). Martyrdom of St. Lucia. Berlin. *(Stoedtner)*
D.   *Filippino Lippi* (1457/8–1504). Vision of St. Bernard (1480). Badia, Florence. *(Stoedtner)*
E.   *Sassetta,* or *Stefano di Giovanni* (1392–1450). The Journey of the Magi. 8½" x 11⅝". MMA, Bequest of Maitland F. Griggs, 1943.
F.   *Giovanni di Paolo* (1402/1403–*c.* 1482). The Presentation in the Temple. 15½" x 18⅛". MMA, Gift of George Blumenthal, 1941.
G.   *Antonio Pisanello* (1395–1455/6). The Vision of St. Eustace (?). 21½" x 25¾". Nat. Gal., London. *(Bruckmann)*

A. *Fra Filippo Lippi* (1406–1469). Dance of Salome. Cathedral, Prato. *(Alinari)*
B. *Masaccio* (1401–1428). The Holy Trinity with the Virgin and St. John (*c.* 1425). Santa Maria Novella, Florence. *(Alinari)*
C. *Paolo Uccello* (1396/7–1475). The Battle of San Romano (*c.* 1455). 72″ x 125″. Nat. Gal., London. *(Arch. Photo.)*
D. *Masaccio.* Expulsion from the Garden (*c.* 1425). 6′9″ x 2′11″. Brancacci Chapel, S. M. del Carmine, Florence. *(Stoedtner)*
E. *Masaccio.* The Tribute Money (*c.* 1425). 19′8″ x 8′4″. Brancacci Chapel, Florence. *(Alinari)*

A.   *Antonello da Messina* (*c.* 1430–1479). The Crucifixion (1475). 23½″ x 16¾″. Roy. Mus. Fine Arts, Antwerp. *(Bruckmann)*
B.   *Piero della Francesca* (1410/20–1492). The Baptism of Christ. 66″ x 45¾″. Nat. Gal., London. *(Mansell)*
C.   *Piero della Francesca.* The Battle of Constantine and Maxentius. San Francesco, Arezzo. *(Alinari)*
D.   *Piero della Francesca.* The Dream of Constantine (*c.* 1455). San Francesco, Arezzo. *(Alinari)*
E.   *Piero della Francesca.* The Resurrection (*c.* 1460). 9′6″ x 8′4″. Picture Gal., Borgo San Sepolcro. *(Alinari)*

A.   *Domenico Ghirlandaio* (1449–1494). The Last Supper (*c.* 1480). *c.* 25′ 7″ wide. San Marco, Florence. *(Stoedtner)*
B. *Andrea del Castagno* (1397–1457). The Last Supper (*c.* 1445–1450). *c.* 28½′ wide. Mus., Sant' Apollonia, Florence. *(Stoedtner)*
C. *Domenico Ghirlandaio.* An Old Man and His Grandson (*c.* 1480). 24½″ x 18″. Louvre. *(Arch. Photo.)*
D. *Bernardino Pinturicchio* (1454–1513). Eneas Piccolomini Leaves for the Council of Basel. Piccolomini Lib., Cathedral, Siena. *(Alinari)*
E. *Benozzo Gozzoli* (1420–1498). Journey of the Magi. *c.* 12′ 4½″. Riccardi Palace, Florence. *(Stoedtner)*
F. *Sandro Botticelli* (1444–1510). Primavera (*c.* 1478). 80″ x 123½″. Uffizi. *(Stoedtner)*

A. *Piero di Cosimo* (*c.* 1462–1521 ?). Simonetta Vespucci (La Bella Simonetta). 22½″ x 16½″. Mus. Condé, Chantilly.
(Arch. Photo.)
B. *Sandro Botticelli* (1444-1510). The Birth of Venus (*c.* 1480). 79″ x 110″. Uffizi. *(ITIO)*
C. *Piero di Cosimo*. Death of Procris. 25¾″ x 72¼″. Nat. Gal., London. *(Mansell)*
D. *Luca Signorelli* (1441–1523). The Damned (*c.* 1500). San Brixio Chapel, Cathedral, Orvieto. *(Alinari)*

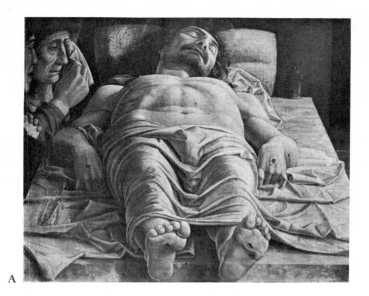

A. *Andrea Mantegna* (*c.* 1431–1506). The Lamentation (*c.* 1490–1500). 27″ x 32″. Brera Gal., Milan. *(Alinari)*
B. *Andrea Mantegna.* Execution of St. James. Chiesa degli Eremitani, Padua. *(Alinari)*
C. *Andrea Mantegna.* Mother and Child. MMA, Whittlesey Fund, 1952.
D. *Andrea Mantegna.* The Battle of the Sea Gods. 11″ high. MMA, Rogers Fund, 1918, 1921.
E. *Antonio del Pollaiuolo* (1432–1498). The Rape of Deinira (*c.* 1475). 21½″ x 31⅝″. Yale Univ. Art. Gal., Jarves Coll.
F. *Antonio del Pollaiuolo.* Battle of Ten Naked Men (*c.* 1465–1470). MMA, Purchase, 1917, Joseph Pulitzer Bequest.

A.   *Carlo Crivelli* (*d.* 1495). Madonna. Brera Gal., Milan. *(Alinari)*
B.   *Gentile Bellini* (1429/30–1507). Miracle of the Cross. Academy, Venice. *(Alinari)*
C.   *Giovanni Bellini* (1430–1516). Pietà (*c.* 1460). Brera Gal., Milan. *(Alinari)*
D.   *Giovanni Bellini*. Allegory in Purgatory (*c.* 1490). 29″ x 47″. Uffizi. *(Alinari)*
E.   *Giovanni Bellini*. St. Francis in Ecstasy (*c.* 1485). 48½″ x 55″. Frick.
F.   *Giovanni Bellini*. Transfiguration (*c.* 1485). 45¼″ x 59⅔″. Nat. Gal., Naples. *(Alinari)*

A

B

C

D

E

A. *Leonardo da Vinci* (1452–1519). The Last Supper (*c.* 1495–1498). 14′5″ x 28′3″. Santa Maria delle Grazie, Milan. *(Alinari)*
B. *Leonardo da Vinci.* The Virgin of the Rocks (*c.* 1485). 74⅝″ x 47¼″. Nat. Gal., London. *(Stoedtner)*
C. *Leonardo da Vinci.* Adoration of the Magi. 95⅝″ x 96⅞″. Uffizi. *(Stoedtner)*
D. *Leonardo da Vinci.* Madonna and St. Anne (1506). 5′7″ x 4′3″. Louvre. *(Stoedtner)*
E. *Leonardo da Vinci.* Lady with a Weasel. 20⅝″ x 16″. Cracow. *(Stoedtner)*

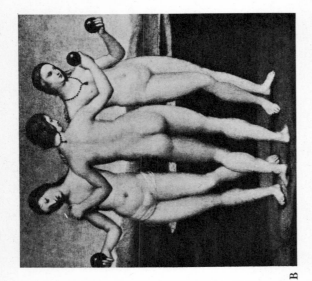

B

D

A

C

A. *Raphael* (1483–1520). St. George and the Dragon. 11⅛″ x 8⁷⁄₁₆″. Nat. Gal, Wash., Mellon Coll, 1937.
B. *Raphael.* The Three Graces. Mus. Condé. *(Stoedtner)*
C. *Raphael.* La Disputa (1509–1511). 18′ x 26′. Camera della Segnatura, Vatican. *(Alinari)*
D. *Raphael.* School of Athens (1508–1513). 18′ x 26′. Camera della Segnatura, Vatican. *(Alinari)*

A. *Raphael* (1483–1520). Galatea (1514). *c.* 7′ 4″ x 9′ 7″. Villa Farnesina, Rome. *(Stoedtner)*
B. *Raphael.* Sistine Madonna (1515). Gemäldegal, Dresden. *(Bruckmann)*
C. *Michelangelo* (1475–1564). Sistine Chapel (1508–1512). Vatican. *(Alinari)*
D. *Michelangelo.* Temptation and Expulsion (1508–1512). More than life size. Sistine Chapel, Vatican. *(Stoedtner)*
E. *Michelangelo.* Isaiah (1508–1512). More than life size. Sistine Chapel, Vatican. *(Stoedtner)*

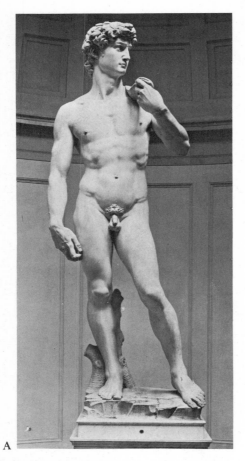

A

B

D

C

E

A.   *Michelangelo* (1475–1564). David (1501–1504). 18′ high. Academy, Florence. *(Alinari)*
B.   *Michelangelo.* Tomb of Lorenzo de' Medici (1524–1534). Width, over all, 12′ 9½″. New Sacristy, San Lorenzo, Florence.
C.   *Michelangelo.* Moses (1513–1515). 8′4″. San Pietro in Vincoli, Rome.
D.   *Michelangelo.* Day—Tomb of Giuliano de' Medici (1524–1534). *c.* 34⅝″ high from base. New Sacristy, San Lorenzo, Florence.
E.   *Michelangelo.* Tomb of Giuliano de' Medici (1524–1534). Central figure, 71″ high. New Sacristy, San Lorenzo, Florence. *(Stoedtner)*

A.   *Michelangelo* (1475–1564). Pietà.St. Peters, Rome. *(Alinari)*
B.   *Michelangelo*. Pietà (unfinished). Cathedral, Florence. *(Stoedtner)*
C. *Michelangelo*. Rondanini Pietà. 77½″ high. Castello Sforzesco, Milan. *(Alinari)*
D.   *Michelangelo*. The Prisoner. Gal., Academy, Florence. *(Alinari)*
E.   *Michelangelo*. The Prisoner. Gal., Academy, Florence. *(Alinari)*

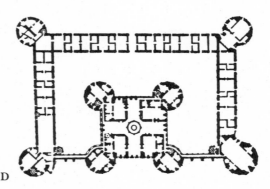

A.   Blois, Château, Louis XII wing (1503).
B.   Blois, Château, Francis I wing (1515–1519). *(FGTO)*
C.   Blois, Château, Francis I wing, stairway. 30′ wide. *(Stoedtner)*
D.   Chambord, Château (1526–1550). 525′ x 370′.
E.   Chambord, Château. *(TWA)*
F.   Chenonceaux, Château (1515). *(FGTO)*

A.   *Lescot* (*c.* 1510–1578). Paris, Louvre, Lescot wing (1541-1548). *c.* 175′ long x 95′ high. *(FGTO)*
B.   *Delorme* (*c.* 1515–1570). Paris, Tuileries, loggia (1564). *(Stoedtner)*
C.   *Primaticcio* (1504–1570). Fontainebleau, Gallery of Francis I (*c.* 1540). 165′ x 20′ x 20′. *(FGTO)*
D.   Fontainebleau, Gallery of Francis I, detail. *(Stoedtner)*
E.   *Serlio* (1475–1554). Ancy-le-Franc, Château (1538–1546). 190′ wide.*(Tour. Club de France)*
F.   Ancy-le-Franc, Château, court. 95′ wide. *(Arch. Photo.)*

A. London, Hampton Court, Palace (1515). *(Stoedtner)*
B. Wollaton Hall (1580–1588). 190′ wide. *(Stoedtner)*
C. Kirby Hall, court (1570). 100′ wide. *(Stoedtner)*
D. Hatfield House (1611). 125′ wide. *(Stoedtner)*
E. Hatfield House, long gallery. 160′ long. *(Stoedtner)*

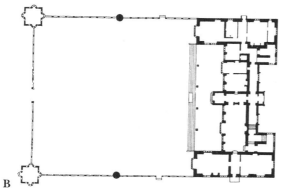

A. Burton Agnes (1602–1610). 137′ wide. *(Country Life)*
B. Montacute House (1580). 160′ x 85′.
C. Sevenoaks, Knole Park, stairs (*c.* 1600). 22′ wide. *(BIS)*
D. Nuremberg, Peller House (1605). *(Stoedtner)*
E. Heidelberg, Castle, Ottoheinrichsbau (1556–1559). *c.* 100′ wide. *(Stoedtner)*

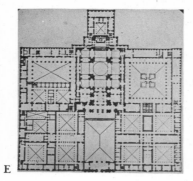

A.   Valladolid, Colegio de San Gregorio, portal (1488–1496). *(Stoedtner)*
B.   *Enrique de Egas* (*c.* 1480–1534). Toledo, Hospital of Santa Cruz, portal (1494–1514). Façade, *c.* 65′ wide. *(Stoedtner)*
C.   *Covarrubias* (*c.* 1488–1564). Salamanca, Palacio Monterey (16th century). *(SNTO)*
D.   *Machuca* (*d.* 1550). Granada. Palace of Charles V, court (begun 1526). 102′ diameter. *(SNTO)*
E.   *Juan Bautista de Toledo* and *Juan de Herrera*. Madrid (near), Escorial (1559–1584). 680′ x 530′.
F.   Madrid, Escorial. *(SNTO)*

A

B

C

D

A.   *Albrecht Dürer* (1471–1528). The Cannon (1518), etching. *(Stoedtner)*
B.   *Lucas van Leyden* (1494–1533), Netherlands School. The Milkmaid, engraving. MMA, Gift of Mrs. Felix Warburg in memory of her husband, Felix M. Warburg, 1941.
C.   *Albrecht Dürer.* Melancholia, engraving. Calif. Palace, Legion of Honor, Achenbach Fund. San Francisco.
D.   *Lucas van Leyden.* Lot and His Daughter. Louvre. *(Arch. Photo.)*

A. *Matthias Grünewald* (*c.* 1485–*c.* 1530). The Crucifixion, upper middle (outer?) section of the Isenheim Altar (1509–1511).
8' 10" x 10' 1". Unterlinden Mus., Colmar, France. *(Bruckmann)*
B. *Matthias Grünewald.* Resurrection of Christ, (inner?) right wing of the Isenheim Altar. *(Bruckmann)*
C. *Matthias Grünewald.* Concert of Angels and Nativity, upper middle (inner?) section of the Isenheim Altar. *(Bruckmann)*

B

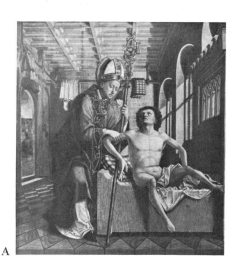

A

C

D

E

A.   *Michael Pacher* (c. 1435–1498). St. Wolfgand and the Thief. Alte Pinakothek, Munich. *(Arch. Photo.)*
B.   *Albrecht Altdorfer* (c. 1480–1538). Birth of Mary. Munich. *(Stoedtner)*
C.   *Anthonis Mor, or Sir Anthony More* (c. 1517/21–1576/7). Portrait of Queen Mary of England. 42⅞″ x 33⅛″. Prado. *(Stoedtner)*
D.   *Hans Baldung Grien* (1480–1545). Three Witches, woodcut. MMA, Gift of Felix M. Warburg and his family, 1941.
E.   *Lucas Cranach the Elder* (1472–1553). The Judgment of Paris. 40⅛″ x 28″. MMA, Rogers Fund, 1928.

A.   *Jan Gossaert,* called *Mabuse* (*d., c.* 1533). Portrait of John Carondelet. Louvre. (*Arch. Photo.*)
B.   *Joachim Patinir* (1475–1524). The River Styx. 25¼″ x 40½″. Prado.
C.   *Hieronymus Bosch* (*c.* 1450–1516). Christ Carrying the Cross. *c.* 29⅝″ x 32⅜″. Mus. Fine Arts, Ghent. (*Arch. Photo.*)
D.   *Hieronymous Bosch.* The Ship of Fools. 22″ x 12⅝″. Louvre. (*Arch. Photo.*)

A

B

C

A. *Pieter Bruegel the Elder* (*c.* 1525–1569). Triumph of Death (*c.* 1564). 46″ x 63¾″. Prado.
B. *Pieter Bruegel the Elder.* Adoration of the Magi (1554?). *c.* 3′ 6½″ x 2′ 8⅔″. Nat. Gal., London. *(Mansell)*
C. *Pieter Bruegel the Elder.* Tower of Babel (1563). 3′8⅞″ x 5′1″. Gemäldegal., Vienna. *(Bruckmann)*

A. *Pieter Bruegel the Elder* (c. 1525–1569). The Return of Hunters (1565). 46" x 63¾". Gemäldegal., Vienna (*Bruckmann*)
B. *Pieter Bruegel the Elder.* The Dark Day. Gemäldegal., Vienna (*Bruckmann*)
C. *Pieter Bruegel the Elder.* The Harvesters (August). 46½" x 63¾". MMA, Rogers Fund, 1919.

A. *Nicholas Hilliard* (*c.* 1547–1619). Unknown Youth Leaning against a Tree of Roses (*c.* 1588). 5⅜″ x 2¾″. Victoria and Albert Mus.
B. *Hans Holbein the Younger* (1497/8–1543). The Ambassadors. 81½″ x 82½″. Nat. Gal., London. *(Stoedtner)*
C. *Hans Holbein the Younger.* The Husbandman—Dance of Death Series (1526), woodcut.
D. *Hans Holbein the Younger.* Portrait Drawing. Windsor Castle. *(Stoedtner)*
E. *Hans Holbein the Younger.* Christine of Denmark. 70½″ x 32½″. Nat. Gal., London. *(Stoedtner)*
F. *Hans Holbein the Younger.* Family of the Artist. 31⁵⁄₁₆″ x 25¹³⁄₁₆″. Kunstmus, Basel. *(Stoedtner)*
G. *Hans Holbein the Younger.* Henry VIII (1540). 32½″ x 29″. Nat. Gal., Rome. *(Stoedtner)*

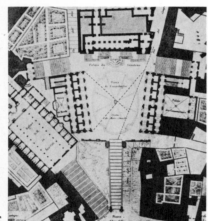

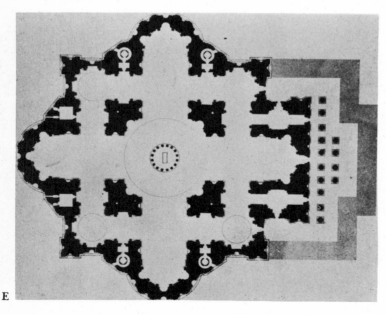

A.   *Ammanati* (1511–1592). Florence, Pitti Palace (1568). Court, 110′ high. *(Stoedtner)*
B.   *Michelangelo* (1475–1564). Florence, Laurentian Library, stairs (1524). *(Stoedtner)*
C.   *Michelangelo.* Rome, Piazza del Campidoglio (begun 1536). *(Stoedtner)*
D.   *Michelangelo.* Rome, Piazza del Campidoglio, Capitoline Museum. 164′ wide. *(Alinari)*
E.   *Michelangelo.* Rome, St. Peter's, plan (1547). *c.* 560′ x 560′. *(Stoedtner)*
F.   *Michelangelo* and *Della Porta* (1537–1604). Rome, St. Peter's, dome, section. *c.* 140′ diameter. *(Stoedtner)*

A.   Rome, St. Peter's. *(Aerofoto)*
B.   Rome, St. Peter's, restored by Conant. Façade as designed by Michelangelo and dome as completed by Della Porta.
C.   *Michelangelo* (1475–1564). Rome, St. Peter's, west end (begun 1547). Total height, 470'.
D.   *Maderna* (1556–1639). Rome, St. Peter's, nave (1606–1626). Total interior length, 710'.

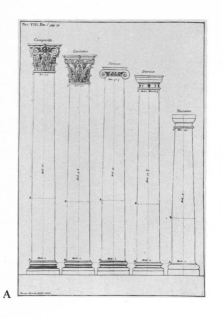

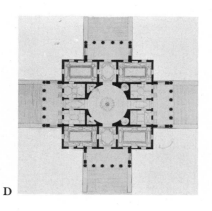

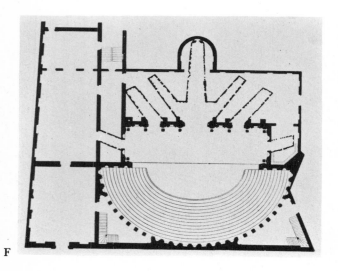

A. *Palladio* (1518–1580). The Five Orders (1570).
B. *Palladio*. Vicenza, Basilica (1549). 232′ x 124′. *(Stoedtner)*
C. *Palladio*. Vicenza, Palazzo Colleoni (1552). 88½′ wide x 59′ high. *(Stoedtner)*
D. *Palladio*. Vicenza, Villa Rotonda (1552). 80′ x 80′. *(Stoedtner)*
E. Vicenza, Villa Rotonda. *(Stoedtner)*
F. *Palladio*. Vicenza, Teatro Olimpico (completed 1584). *(Stoedtner)*
G. Vicenza, Teatro Olimpico. Stage, 230′ wide. *(Stoedtner)*

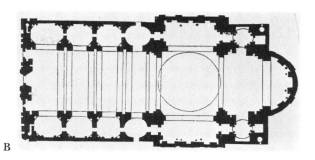

A.   *Vignola* (1507–1573). Rome, Villa di Papa Giulio (1550). 90′ diameter of exedra. *(Stoedtner)*
B.   *Vignola.* Rome, Il Gesù (1568–1584). Interior, 225′ x 115′. *(Stoedtner)*
C.   Rome, Il Gesù. *(Stoedtner)*
D.   *Della Porta* (1537–1604). Rome, Il Gesù, façade. *c.* 115′ x 114′ high. *(Stoedtner)*
E.   Bagnaia, Villa Lante. *(Stoedtner)*
F.   Bagnaia, Villa Lante. *(Stoedtner)*

A

B

C

A. *Michelangelo* (1475–1564). Last Judgment (1534–1541). End wall, Sistine Chapel. *(Alinari)*
B. *Francesco Parmigianino* (1503–1540). Madonna with the Long Neck (*c.* 1535). 85″ x 52″. Uffizi. *(Alinari)*
C. *Jacopo Pontormo* (1494–1556). Descent from the Cross (1525–1528). 123″ x 75½″. Santa Felicità, Florence. *(Alinari)*

A.   *Dosso Dossi* (*c.* 1479?–1542). Circe and Her Lovers in a Landscape. 39⅝″ x 53½″. Nat. Gal., Wash., Samuel H. Kress Coll.
B.   *Angelo Bronzino* (1503–1572). Portrait of a Young Man. 37⅝″ x 29½″. MMA, Bequest of Mrs. H. O. Havemeyer, 1929, the H. O. Havemeyer Coll.
C.   *Michelangelo da Caravaggio* (1573–1610). Entombment. *c.* 9′ 10-1/16″ x 6′ 8″. Vatican. *(Alinari)*
D.   *Michelangelo da Caravaggio.* Bacchus (*c.* 1590). 38½″ x 33½″. Uffizi. *(Alinari)*
E.   *Michelangelo da Caravaggio.* St. Matthew and the Angel (1597). Church of San Liugi dei Francesi, Rome. *(Alinari)*
F.   *Antonio Correggio* (1494–1534). Jupiter and Io (*c.* 1530). 5′4″ x 2′5″. Vienna. *(Stoedtner)*
G.   *Antonio Correggio.* Assumption (1520–1524). Dome, Cathedral, Parma *(Stoedtner)*

A. *Giorgione* (1476/8–1510). The Madonna. Castelfranco. *(Alinari)*
B. *Giorgione*. Pastoral Symphony (late, *c.* 1510). 43¼″ x 54⅜″. Louvre. *(MMA)*
C. *Giorgione* and *Titian* (1477–1576). The Concert (*c.* 1510). 40″ x 48″. Pitti Palace, Florence. *(Alinari)*
D. *Giorgione*. The Tempest (*c.* 1505). 32¼″ x 28¾″. Academy, Venice. *(Alinari)*

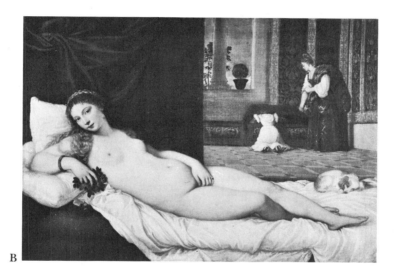

A. *Giorgione* (1476/8–1510). Sleeping Venus (*c.* 1508–1510). 3′7″ x 5′9″. Gemäldegal, Dresden. (*Bruckmann*)
B. *Titian* (1477–1576). Venus. *c.* 47″ x 65″. Uffizi. (*Alinari*)
C. *Titian*. Sacred and Profane Love. *c.* 46½″ x 110″. Borghese Gal., Rome. (*Alinari*)

A

B

C

D

E

A.   *Titian* (1477–1576). Madonna with Member of the Pesaro Family (1526). 16′ x 8′10″. Church of the Frari, Venice. *(Alinari)*
B.   *Titian.* Self-portrait (*c.* 1550). 38″ x 29½″. Kaiser Friedrich Mus., Berlin *(Bruckmann)*
C.   *Titian.* Paul III and His Nephews (1546). 78½″ x 49″. Nat. Mus., Naples. *(Alinari)*
D.   *Titian.* Portrait of Charles V. 10′10¾″ x 8′1⅞″. Prado. *(Bruckmann)*
E.   *Titian.* A Bacchanalian Festival (*c.* 1518). 68⅞″ x 76″. Prado. *(Bruckmann)*

A.   *Titian* (1477–1576). Nymph and Satyr. Gemäldegal., Vienna. *(Bruckmann)*
B.   *Titian*. Christ Crowned with Thorns (*c.* 1565). 110″ x 72″. Pinakothek, Munich. *(Bruckmann)*
C.   *Titian*. Entombment (1559). 53⅞″ x 68⅞″. Prado. *(Foto Manso)*
D.   *Paolo Veronese* (1528–1588). Christ in the House of Levi (1573). 18′2″ x 42′. Academy, Venice. *(Alinari)*

A. *Paolo Veronese* (1528–1588). Venus and Adonis (*c.* 1580). 83½″ x 75¼″. Prado. (*Foto Manso*)
B. *Jacopo Tintoretto* (1518–1594). St. Mary of Egypt (1583–1587). 13′ 11″ x 6′ 11″. San Rocco, Venice. (*Alinari*)
C. *Jacopo Tintoretto.* Susanna and the Elders. 56½″ x 76″. Gemäldegal., Vienna. (*Bruckmann*)
D. *Jacopo Tintoretto.* Christ Carrying the Cross. 17′ 1″ x 13′ 3½″. San Rocco, Venice. (*Alinari*)
E. *Jacopo Tintoretto.* The Last Supper (1592–1594). 12′ x 18′8″. San Giorgio Maggiore, Venice. (*Frick*)

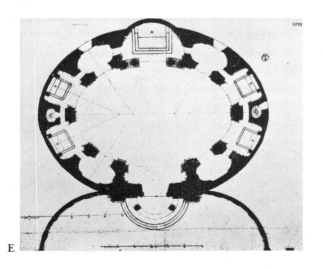

A.   *Maderna* (1556–1639). Rome, Acqua Paola (1611). 95′ 9″ wide. *(Stoedtner)*
B.   *Maderna.* Rome, Sta Suzanna (1600). *(Stoedtner)*
C. *Bernini* (1598–1680). Rome, St. Peter's, colonnades (1667). Breadth of ellipse, 780′. *(Alinari)*
D.   *Bernini.* Rome, Vatican, Scala Regia (1663–1666). 200′ deep. *(Stoedtner)*
E.   *Bernini.* Rome, Sant' Andrea al Quirinale (1658–1670). *c.* 115′ x 100′.
F.   Rome, Sant' Andrea al Quirinale. *(Alinari)*

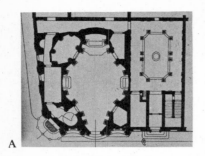

A

B

C

D

E

F

A.   *Borromini* (1599–1667). Rome, San Carlo alle Quattro Fontane (1638–1667). Interior of Church, 52′ 6″ x 34′. *(Stoedtner)*
B.   Rome, San Carlo alle Quattro Fontane. *(Alinari)*
C.   Rome, San Carlo alle Quattro Fontane, cloister. *(Alinari)*
D.   Rome, San Carlo alle Quattro Fontane, façade. 38′ wide. *(Stoedtner)*
E.   *Borromini.* Rome, Sant' Ivo section (1642–1650). *c.* 85′, maximum diameter. *(Stoedtner)*
F.   *Borromini.* Rome, Palazzo Spada, gallery (1632). 27′ deep. *(Alinari)*

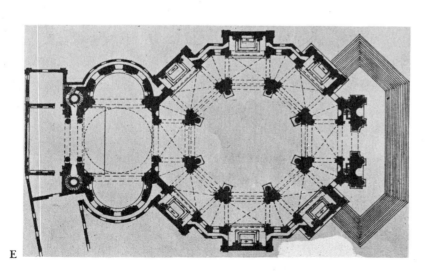

A.   *Borromini* (1599–1667). Rome, Sant' Agnese, façade (begun 1652). *c.* 160' wide. *(Stoedtner)*
B.   *Cortona* (1596–1669). Rome, Santa Maria della Pace (1656–1657). 51' wide. *(Stoedtner)*
C.   *Salvi* (1697–1751). Rome, Trevi Fountain (1735–1762). 151' wide. *(Stoedtner)*
D.   *Gherardi* (1644–1702). Rome, Santa Maria in Trastevere, Avila Chapel, cupola (before 1686). *(Alinari)*
E.   *Longhena* (1598–1682). Venice, Santa Maria della Salute (1631–1682). *c.* 200' x 155'. *(Stoedtner)*
F.   Venice, Santa Maria della Salute. *(Stoedtner)*

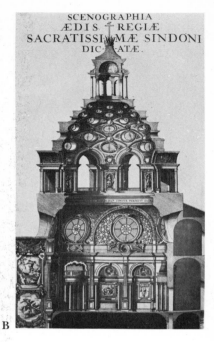

A.   *Galilei* (1691–1737). Rome, St. John Lateran, façade (1734). *c.* 200′ wide. *(ISTO)*
B.   *Guarini* (1624–1683). Turin, Sma Sindone, section (1667–1690). *(Stoedtner)*
C.   Turin, Sma Sindone. *(Stoedtner)*
D.   Turin, Sma Sindone. *(Alinari)*
E.   *Juvara* (1678–1736). Turin, La Superga (1717–1731). *c.* 115′ high. *(ISTO)*

A.   *Neumann* (1687–1753). Vierzehnheiligen, façade (1743–1772). 361′ wide. *(Marburg)*
B.   *Prandtauer* (1660–1726). Melk, Klosterkirche (1701–1738). *(Marburg)*
C.   *Pöppelmann* (1662–1736). Dresden, Zwinger, pavilion (1711–1722). *(Stoedtner)*
D.   *Luis de Arévalo* and *E. Manuel Vasquez.* Granada, Cartuja, sacristy (1727–1764). *(Stoedtner)*
E.   Léon, San Marcos, façade.
F.   *Ribera* (c. 1683–1742). Madrid, Hospicio Provincial, façade (1772).

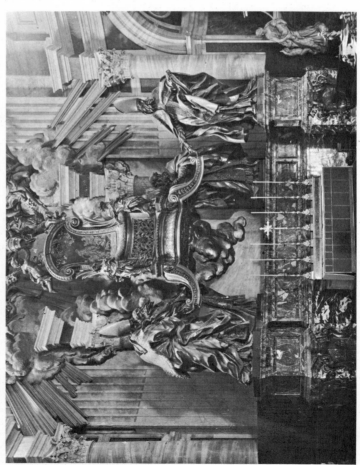

A. *Giovanni Bologna* (1529–1608). Rape of the Sabines (1579–1583). Loggia de' Lanzi, Florence. (*Stoedtner*)
B. *Gianlorenzo Bernini* (1598–1680). Rape of Proserpina. *c.* 8½' high. Borghese Gal., Rome. (*Stoedtner*)
C. *Gianlorenzo Bernini*. Louis XIV. 33⅛" high. Nat. Gal., Wash., Kress Coll.
D. *Gianlorenzo Bernini*. Throne of St. Peter (1657–1666). Apse, St. Peter's, Rome. (*Alinari*)
E. *Gianlorenzo Bernini*. Monument of Alexander VII. Basilica of St. Peter's, Rome. (*Alinari*)

A

B

C

D

A.   *Guercino* (1591–1666). Burial of St. Petronilla (1621). 23′7″ x 13′10″. Capitoline Mus. *(Alinari)*
B.   *Giambattista Piranesi* (1720–1778). The Prisons, plate III, first state. MMA, Dick Fund, 1937.
C.   *Giovanni Battista Tiepolo* (1696–1770, Venetian School). Last Supper. *c.* 31¹¹/₁₆″ x 34⅝″. Louvre. *(Arch. Photo.)*
D. *Alessandro Longhi* (1773–1813, Venetian School). Exhibition of the Rhinoceros at Venice. *c.* 23¾″ x 18½″. Nat. Gal., London.

A

B

C

D

E

F

A.   *Francesco Guardi* (1712–1793, Venetian School). Doge Embarking (*c.* 1763). 26⅜″ x 39⅜″. Louvre. *(Arch. Photo.)*
B.   *Giovanni Battista Tiepolo* (1696–1770, Venetian School). Car of Venus (El Olimpo). *c.* 33-15/16″ x 24½″. Prado. *(Bruckmann)*
C.   *Antonio Canaletto,* or *Bernardo Bellotto* (1697–1768). View of Venice. Munich. *(Bruckmann)*
D.   *Bermejo.* Virgin with Dead Christ. Cathedral, Barcelona. *(Arch. Photo.)*
E.   *El Greco* (1541–1614). Expulsion from the Temple. 16½″ x 20⅝″. Frick.
F.   *Unknown artist.* Martyrdom of St. Cugat (16th century, Catalonian School). Mus. de Arte, Barcelona.

A.   *El Greco* (1541–1614). View of Toledo (*c.* 1604–1614). 47¾″ x 42¾″. MMA, Bequest of Mrs. H. O.
     Havemeyer, 1929, the H. O. Havemeyer Fund.
B.   *El Greco.* The Adoration of the Shepherds. 64½″ x 42″. MMA, Rogers Fund, 1905.
C.   *El Greco.* Resurrection (1595–1600). 9′ x 4′2″. Prado. *(SNTO)*
D.   *El Greco.* Burial of the Count of Orgaz (1586). 15′9″ x 11′9″. Santo Tomé, Toledo. *(SNTO)*

A

B

C

D

E

A.   *Diego Velásquez* (1599–1660). Los Borrachos. 65-15/16″ x 88⅝″. Prado
B.   *Diego Velásquez.* The Spinners (1656). *c.* 7′3⅜″ x 9′5¾″. Prado. *(SNTO)*
C.   *Diego Velásquez.* Venus and Cupid (1651). 48¼″ x 69¾″. Nat. Gal., London.
D.   *Diego Velásquez.* Surrender of Breda (1634–1635). 10′1″ x 12′. Prado. *(SNTO)*
E.   *Diego Velásquez.* The Maids of Honor (1656). 10′5″ x 9′. Prado. *(SNTO)*

A

B

C

E

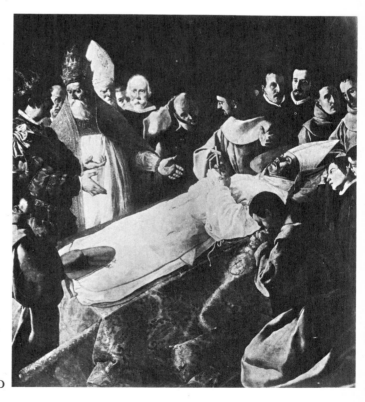

D

A. *Diego Velásquez* (1599–1660). Villa Medici Gardens (1649–1660). 18⅞″ x 16½″. Prado. *(SNTO)*
B. *Diego Velásquez.* The Infanta Maria Theresa. 87¹⁄₁₆″ x 57¹³⁄₁₆″. Prado. *(Bruckmann)*
C. *Bartolomé Esteban Murillo* (1617–1682). Immaculate Conception (1678). 107⅞″ x 74¾″. Prado. *(SNTO)*
D. *Francisco de Zurbarán* (1598–1664). Funeral of St. Bonaventure. 98¾″ x 86⅝″. Louvre. *(Arch. Photo.)*
E. *José Ribera* (1591–1652). Martyrdom of St. Bartholomew (1639?). 92⅛″ x 92⅛″. Prado. *(SNTO)*

A. *Francisco Goya* (1746–1828). Maja Clothed (*c*. 1797–1798). 37⅜″ x 74¾″. Prado. *(Alinari)*
B. *Francisco Goya.* Maja Nude (*c*. 1797–1798). 37⅜″ x 74¾″. Prado. *(Alinari)*
C. *Francisco Goya.* Family of Charles IV (1800). 110″ x 132″. Prado. *(Alinari)*
D. *Francisco Goya.* Madhouse. Acad. de San Fernando, Madrid. *(SNTO)*
E. *Francisco Goya.* The Repentant Peter (1824–1825). 29″ x 25½″. Phillips Coll., Wash.
F. *Francisco Goya.* The Third of May, 1808 (1814–1815) 8′9″ x 13′4″. Prado. *(SNTO)*

A. *Francisco Goya* (1746–1828). Disasters of War, Pl. 30 (Ravages of War). MMA.
B. *Francisco Goya.* Proverbs, Pl. 10 (Woman and Horse). *(Stoedtner)*
C. *Francisco Goya.* Witches' Sabbath (*c.* 1819–1823). 55⅛″ x 172½″. Prado. *(SNTO)*
D. *Peter Paul Rubens* (1577–1640). Rape of the Daughters of Leucippus (*c.* 1618). 7′3″ x 6′10″. Pinakothek. *(Bruckmann)*
E. *Peter Paul Rubens.* Descent from the Cross (1611–1614). 13′10″ x 10′1″. Cathedral, Antwerp. *(Bruckmann)*

B

D

A

C

A. *Peter Paul Rubens* (1577–1640). Landscape with Chateau of Steen (1636). 54" x 92½". Nat. Gal., London.
B. *Peter Paul Rubens*. Landing of Marie de Médicis at Marseilles (1621–1640). *c.* 12' 11⅛" x 9' 8⅛". Louvre. (*Arch. Photo*)
C. *Peter Paul Rubens*, Lion Hunt (1616–1621). Pinokothek. (*Bruckmann*)
D. *Peter Paul Rubens*. Quos Ego (1634). 19¼" x 25¼". Fogg.

A

B

C

D

A. *Peter Paul Rubens* (1577–1640). Helena Fourment. Gemäldegal., Vienna. *(Bruckmann)*
B. *Peter Paul Rubens.* Helena Fourment (*c.* 1620). 30½″ x 21″. Nat. Gal., London. *(Bruckmann)*
C. *Anthony Van Dyck* (1599–1641). John and Bernard Stuart (*c.* 1638). Cobham Hall. *(Stoedtner)*
D. *Anthony Van Dyck.* Cardinal Bentivoglio (1623). Pitti Palace. *(Alinari)*

A. Jacob Jordaens (1593–1678). The King Drinks (c. 1638). 59⅛″ x 82¾″. Roy. Mus. Fine Arts, Brussels.
B. Adriaen Brouwer 1605/6–1688). The Smoker (1638?). 16⅛″ x 12⅝″. Louvre. (Arch. Photo.)
C. Adriaen Brouwer. Brawl over a Game of Cards. Gemäldegal., Dresden. (Bruckmann)
D. David Teniers the Younger (1610–1690). Village Festival. 26¾″ x 39¾″. MMA, Bequest of Collis P. Huntington, 1925.

A

B

C

D

E

A.   *Jan Steen* (*c.* 1626–1679). The Lovesick Maiden. 34″ x 39″. MMA, Bequest of Helen B. Neilson, 1945.
B.   *Gerard Terborch* (1617–1681). Paternal Admonition. Berlin. *(Bruckmann)*
C.   *Frans Hals* (1580/5–1666). Portrait of Willem van Heythuryen (1630's?). 18-3/10″ x 14-4/5″. Roy. Mus. Fine Arts, Brussels
(Bruckmann)
D.   *Frans Hals.* Malle Babbe (*c.* 1650). 29½″ x 25″. MMA, Purchase, 1871.
E.   *Frans Hals.* The Women Regents of the Old Men's Home (*c.* 1664). 67″ x 98″. Frans Hals Mus., Haarlem. *(Stoedtner)*

A. *Meindert Hobbema* (1638–1709). Landscape of Middleharnis (1689). 40½″ x 55½″. Nat. Gal., London. *(Stoedtner)*
B. *Jacob van Ruisdael* (1628–1682). The Mill Near Wisk. 2′9″ x 3′4″. Rijksmus., Amsterdam.
C. *Jacob van Ruisdael.* A View of Haarlem (*c.* 1660). Rijksmus. *(NIO, photo Adrien Boutrelle)*
D. *Jacob van Ruisdael.* Winter. Rijksmus. *(Stoedtner)*
E. *Jacob van Ruisdael.* Jewish Cemetery (*c.* 1660). 56″ x 74¼″. Detroit Inst. Arts.

A

B

C

D

E

A.   *Willem I. van de Velde* (1611–1693). The Cannon Shot. Rijksmus. *(Stoedtner)*
B.   *Willem Kalf* (1622–1695). Still Life (1659). 30″ x 23″. MMA, Maria De Witt Jesup Fund, 1953.
C.   *Albert Cuyp* (1620–1691). Cows in Water. Budapest. *(Stoedtner)*
D.   *Paulus Potter* (1625–1654). The Young Bull (1647). Mauritshuis, The Hague. *(NIO)*
E.   *Carel Fabritius* (1622–1654). The Goldfinch (1654). 13″ x 8⅝″. The Hague. *(Stoedtner)*

A   *Hercules Seghers* (1589-1638). The Big Ships, etching. Staats. Kunst., Dresden.
B.   *Rembrandt van Rijn* (1606–1669). Goldweigher's Field, etching. MMA.
C.   *Rembrandt van Rijn*. Christ Presented to the People (1655). Etching, first state. MMA, Gift of Felix Warburg and his family, 1941.
D.   *Rembrandt van Rijn*. Christ Presented to the People, detail. MMA.
E.   *Rembrandt van Rijn*. Woman with Arrow, etching. *(Stoedtner)*
F.   *Rembrandt van Rijn*. A Girl Sleeping (*c.* 1655–1656), drawing. 9⅔″ x 8″. Brit. Mus.
G.   *Rembrandt van Rijn*. Saskia Carrying Rumbartus Downstairs, drawing. Morgan Lib.

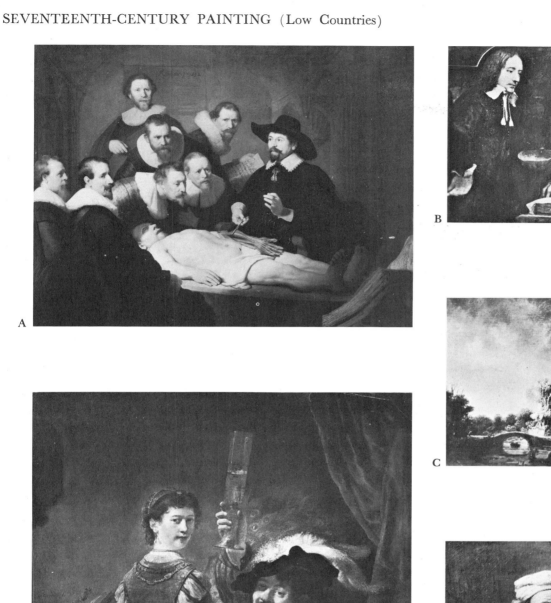

A. *Rembrandt van Rijn* (1606–1669). The Anatomy Lesson of Dr. Tulp (1632). 66¾″ x 85¼″. Mauritshuis. *(© Foto-Administralie)*
B. *Rembrandt van Rijn.* The Anatomical Lesson of Dr. Deyman (1656). 40″ x 52″. Rijksmus.
C. *Rembrandt van Rijn.* The Stone Bridge. *c.* 11⅝″ x 16¾″. Rijksmus.
D. *Rembrandt van Rijn.* Self-portrait with His Wife Saskia (*c.* 1634). 64″ x 52″. Gemäldegal., Dresden. *(Bruckmann)*
E. *Rembrandt van Rijn.* Self-portrait at the Easel (1660). 44″ x 34″. Louvre. *(Arch. Photo.)*

A.   *Rembrandt van Rijn* (1606–1669). The Night Watch (1642). 12′2″ x 14′7″. Rijksmus. *(NIO)*
B.   *Rembrandt van Rijn.* Return of the Prodigal Son (*c.* 1669). 103⅛″ x 80⅝″. Hermitage, Leningrad.
C.   *Rembrandt van Rijn.* The Jewish Bride . 47″ x 65½″. Rijksmus.
D.   *Rembrandt van Rijn.* Beef Carcass (*c.* 1655). 28½″ x 20½″. Louvre. *(Arch Photo.)*

A

B

C

D

E

A.   *Rembrandt van Rijn* (1606–1669). Jan Six (1654). 44½″ x 40″. Six Coll., Amsterdam. *(Stoedtner)*
B.   *Rembrandt van Rijn*. Family Portrait (*c.* 1668). 50″ x 66½″. Mun. Mus., Brunswick, Germany. *(Stoedtner)*
C.   *Rembrandt van Rijn*. Woman Bathing. 24-5/16″ x 18½″. Nat. Gal., London. *(Stoedtner)*
D.   *Jan Vermeer* (1632–1675). The Artist in His Studio (*c.* 1665–1670). 52″ x 44″. Kunsthist. Mus., Vienna.
E.   *Jan Vermeer*. Milkmaid. 18⅛″ x 16-1/16″. Rijksmus. *(NIO)*

A

D

B

C

E

A. *Jan Vermeer* (1632–1675). Music Master and Pupil at Spinet. 29″ x 25″. Windsor Castle. *(Stoedtner)*
B. *Pieter de Hooch* (1629–1677). Interior with Card Players (1658). 30″ x 26½″. Buckingham Palace. *(Stoedtner)*
C. *Pieter de Hooch.* Lady with Maid on a Roof (1672). 29″ x 24⅝″. Nat. Gal., London. *(Stoedtner)*
D. *Jan Vermeer.* The Letter. 17¼″ x 15½″. Rijksmus. *(Bruckmann)*
E. *Jan Vermeer.* The Little Street in Delft (c. 1660). 21¾″ x 17″. Rijksmus. *(OTIO, © Fotographie)*

A

B

D

C

E

A.   *Pieter Jans Saenredam* (1597–1665). Panel. 50-11/16″ x 34¼″. Cathedral of St. John at 'S-Hertogenbosch.
Nat. Gal., Wash., Kress Coll.
B.   *Jan Vermeer* (1632–1675). View of Delft. 39″ x 46½″. Mauritshuis. *(NIO)*
C.   Paris, Place des Vosges (early 17th century). *(Stoedtner)*
D.   *De Brosse* (c. 1555–1626). Paris, Luxembourg, garden front (1615–1620). *c.* 300′ wide. *(Stoedtner)*
E.   *Le Mercier* (1590–1660.) Paris, Louvre, Pavillon de l'Horloge (1624–1630), *c.* 60′ wide. *(Stoedtner)*

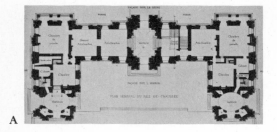

A

B

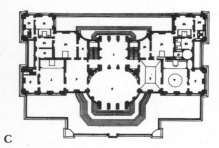

C

D

E

F

G

A.   *F. Mansart* (1598–1666). Maisons-Laffitte, Château (1642–1651). *c.* 235′ x 117′. *(Stoedtner)*
B.   Maisons-Laffitte, Château, court of honor. *(Stoedtner)*
C.   *Le Vau* (1612–1670). Vaux-le-Vicomte, Château (1657–1660). 235′ x 125′. *(Stoedtner)*
D.   Vaux-le-Vicomte, Château, garden front. *(Stoedtner)*
E.   *F. Mansart.* Paris, Val de Grâce (1645–1666). 133′ high. *(French Embassy)*
F.   *Blondel* (1617–1686). Paris, Porte St. Denis (1672). 81′ high. *(Stoedtner)*
G.   *J. H. Mansart* (1645–1708). Paris, Les Invalides (1706). 198′ wide x 344′ high. *(French Embassy)*

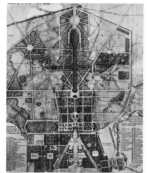

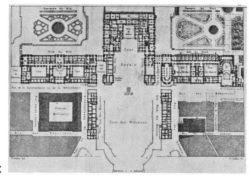

A. *Perrault* (1613–1688). Paris, Louvre, east front (1667–1674). 570′ long x 90′ high. *(Stoedtner)*
B. Versailles, Palace and Park, plot plan. *(Stoedtner)*
C. Versailles, Palace, plan (1661–1756). 1903′ long. *(Stoedtner)*
D. Versailles, Palace, Cour de Marbre, detail. *(Stoedtner)*
E. *Le Vau* and *J. H. Mansart*. Versailles, Palace, Cour d'Honneur.

A. *J. H. Mansart* (1645–1708). Versailles, Palace, garden front. *(FGTO)*
B. Versailles, Palace, Queen's Staircase. *(Stoedtner)*
C. *J. H. Mansart,* architect, and *Le Brun* (1619–1690), decorator. Versailles, Palace,
Hall of Mirrors (1678–1684). 240′ x 34′ x 43′ high. *(FGTO)*
D. Versailles, Palace, Hall of Mirrors, detail. *(Alinari)*
E. Versailles, Palace, Chapel. *(FGTO, photo © Marcil)*

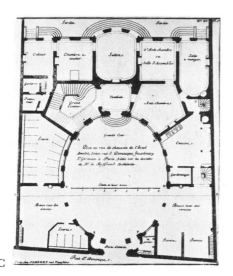

A. *Boffrand* (1667–1754). Paris, Hôtel de Soubise, Salon de la Princesse (*c.* 1740). *c.* 33′ x 26′. *(Stoedtner)*
B. Paris, Hôtel de Soubise, Salon de la Princesse, detail. *(Stoedtner)*
C. *Boffrand.* Paris, Hôtel d'Amelot (1695). *c.* 60′ x 75′. *(Stoedtner)*
D. *Gabriel* (1698-1782). Versailles, Petit Trianon (1762-1768). 78′ 6″ wide x 37′ high.
E. Nancy, Place Stanislas, gate (1752–1755). *(FGTO, photo © Karquel)*
F. *Gabriel.* Paris, Ministry of Marine (1762–1770). 75′ high. *(Stoedtner)*

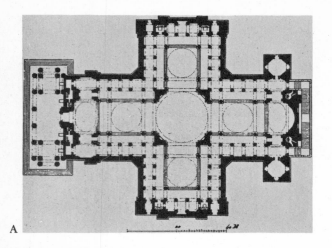

A.   *Soufflot* (1709–1780). Paris, Panthéon (1764–1790). 360′ x 262′. *(Stoedtner)*
B.   Paris, Panthéon. 265′ high. *(Stoedtner)*
C.   Paris, Panthéon, interior. *(French Embassy)*
D.   *The Limburg Brothers.* Temptation and Expulsion from *Très riches heures* (1416). Bib. Nat., Paris. *(Stoedtner)*
E.   *Master of Le Coeur d'Amour épris.* Fol. 12: Magic Fountain. Vienna *(Stoedtner)*
F.   *Southern French master.* The Avignon Pietà (*c.* 1470). 64″ x 86″. Louvre. *(Arch. Photo.)*

A

B

C

D

E

A.   *Jean Fouquet* (*c.* 1420–1481 or earlier). Book of Hours (*c.* 1450). 6½″ x 4¾″. Mus. Condé. *(Arch. Photo.)*
B.   *The Limburg Brothers.* February, from *Très riches heures du Duc de Berri* (1416). Mus. Condé. *(MMA)*
C.   *Jean Fouquet.* Madonna and Child (*c.* 1450). 37⅜″ x 33⅛″. Antwerp. *(Stoedtner)*
D.   *Enguerrand Charanton, or Quarton* (*c.* 1410-*c.* 1461). Coronation of the Virgin (1454). Antwerp. *(Stoedtner)*
E.   *François Clouet* (*c.* 1505–1572). Elizabeth of Austria (c. 1525–1530). 14″ x 10″. Bib. Nat., Paris. *(Arch. Photo.)*

A

B

C

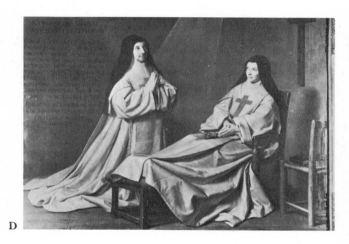

D

E

A.   *François Clouet* (*c.* 1505–1572). Portrait of Francis I (*c.* 1542). Uffizi. *(Alinari)*
B.   *Giovanni Battista Rosso* (1495–1540). Painting and sculpture, Gal. of Francis I, Fontainebleau. *(Arch. Photo.)*
C.   *Anon.* Man with Glass of Wine (1456). *c.* 24¾″ x 17⁵⁄₁₆″. Louvre. *(Arch. Photo.)*
D.   *Philippe de Champaigne* (1602–1674). Mother Catherine Arnauld and Sister Catherine of St. Susanna (1662). 65″ x 90″. Louvre.
(French Cult. Serv.)
E.   *Louis Le Nain* (*c.* 1593–1648). Peasants' Meal. *c.* 38-3/16″ x 48″. Louvre. *(French Cult. Serv.)*

A.   *Mathieu Le Nain* (*c.* 1607–1677). The Forge (before 1648). Reims. *(Arch. Photo.)*
B.   *Georges de la Tour* (1593–1652). Joseph the Carpenter (*c.* 1645). 38½″ x 28½″. Louvre. *(Arch. Photo.)*
C.   *Jacques Callot* (1592–1634). Two Pantaloons, etching. MMA, Dick Fund, 1928.
D.   *Nicolas Poussin* (1593/4–1665). Self-portrait (*c.* 1650). 38½″ x 28¾″. Louvre. *(Arch. Photo.)*
E.   *Nicolas Poussin.* Landscape with the Burial of Phocion (1648). 47″ x 70½″. Louvre. *(Arch. Photo.)*

A. *Nicolas Poussin* (1593/4–1665). Summer (1660–1664). *c.* 46⁷⁄₁₆″ x 63″. Louvre. *(Arch. Photo.)*
B. *Nicolas Poussin.* Autumn. *c.* 46⁷⁄₁₆″ x 63″. Louvre. *(Arch. Photo.)*
C. *Claude Lorrain* (1600–1682). Cleopatra Disembarking at Tarus (*c.* 1647). 3′10¾″ x 5′6½″. Louvre. *(Arch. Photo.)*
D. *Claude Lorrain.* Landscape by the Sea, with Acis and Galatea. *(Stoedtner)*
E. *Claude Lorrain.* View of the Campagna (*c.* 1650?), wash drawing. Brit. Mus. *(Mansell)*

A. *Jean Antoine Watteau* (1684–1721). Drawing for Mezzetin. 17″ x 21¾″. MMA, Munsey Fund, 1934.
B. *Jean Antoine Watteau.* Mezzetin. 5⅛″ x 5⅞″. MMA, Roger's Fund, 1937.
C. *Jean Antoine Watteau.* Gersaint's signboard: Packing of Pictures (1720). 64″ x 121″. Berlin. *(Stoedtner)*
D. *Jean Antoine Watteau.* Gersaint's signboard: Sales (1720). 64″ x 121″. Berlin. *(Stoedtner)*
E. *Jean Antoine Watteau.* Embarkation for Cythera (1717). 4′ 3″ x 6′ 4″. Louvre. *(Stoedtner)*
F. *Jean Antoine Watteau.* Nymph and Satyr. 22″ x 43″. Louvre. *(Arch. Photo.)*
G. *Jean Baptiste Pater* (1695–1736). The Bath. Berlin. *(Stoedtner)*

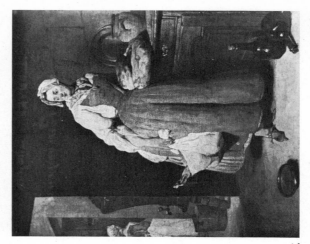

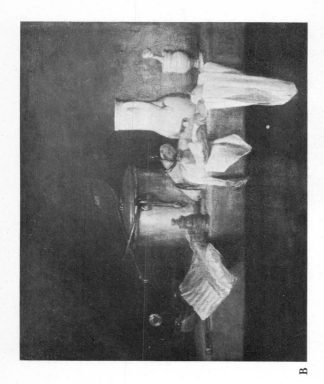

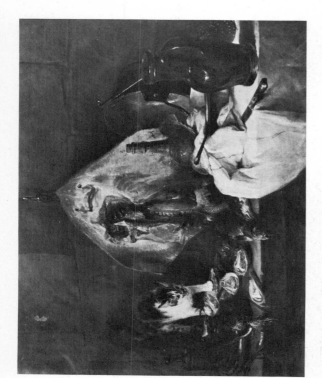

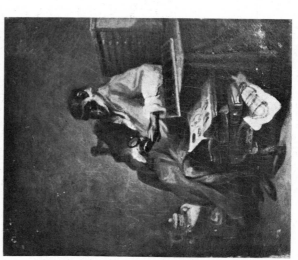

A. *Jean Baptiste Siméon Chardin* (1699–1779). The Ray (c. 1728). 43" x 55". Louvre. *(Arch. Photo.)*
B. *Jean Baptiste Siméon Chardin.* Still Life: Kitchen Table (1733). 12" x 13". MFA.
C. *Jean Baptiste Siméon Chardin.* The Monkey Antiquarian (c. 1736). 16¼" x 12¼". Chartres. *(Arch. Photo.)*
D. *Jean Baptiste Siméon Chardin.* The Copper Cistern (1737). 9" x 8½". Louvre. *(Arch. Photo.)*
E. *Jean Baptiste Siméon Chardin.* Housewife (1739). 18⅛" x 14⅝". Louvre. *(Arch. Photo.)*

A. *François Boucher* (1703–1770). Mlle O'Murphy. Pinakothek. *(Bruckmann)*
B. *Jean Honoré Fragonard* (1732–1806). The Bathers (*c.* 1765). 25¼″ x 31½″. Louvre. *(Arch. Photo.)*
C. *Jean Honoré Fragonard.* The Rendezvous (1773). *c.* 12½″ x 9½″. Frick.
D. *Jean Honoré Fragonard.* The Storm, or The Hay Cart. *c.* 28¾″ x 38″. Louvre. *(Arch. Photo.)*
E. *Jean Baptiste Greuze* (1725–1805). The Village Bride (1761). 36″ x 46½″. Louvre. *(Arch. Photo.)*
F. *Hubert Robert* (1733–1808). Cascades of Tivoli. *c.* 29½″ x 23⅝″. Louvre. *(Arch. Photo.)*

A.   *Maurice Quentin de La Tour* (1704–1788). J. J. Rousseau. Mus. San Quentin. *(Bulloz)*
B.   *Pierre Mignard* (1610–1695). Portrait of Molière in Caesar's Costume. *(Stoedtner)*
C.   *Elisabeth Vigée-Lebrun* (1755–1842). Marie Antoinette (1779). Château de Versailles. *(Alinari)*
D.   *Hyacinthe Rigaud* (1659–1743). Louis XIV (1701). 9'1⅞" x 6'2¾". Louvre. *(Arch. Photo.)*
E.   *François Boucher* (1703–1770). Marquise de Pompadour. Nat. Gal., Edinburgh. *(Mansell)*
F.   *Jean Antoine Houdon* (1741–1828). Voltaire. Life size. Louvre. *(Arch. Photo.)*

A.   *Jean Goujon* (*fl.* 1540–1562). Nymphs, Fountain of the Innocents (1548–1549). Approx. life size. Paris.
(*French Cult. Serv.; photo Bulloz*)
B.   *Anon.* Calvary (1602), granite. Plougastel, Brittany. (*Arch. Photo.*)
C.   *Pierre Puget* (1620–1694). Milo de Crotona (1671–1683). Louvre. (*French Cult. Serv.; photo Bulloz*)
D.   *Guillaume Coustou* (1677–1746). One of the Horses of Marly (1740–1745). Place de la Concorde, Paris. (*Arch. Photo.*)

A.   *Jean Baptiste Pigalle* (1714–1785). Tomb of the Maréchal de Saxe (1753–1776), marble. 15′11″ high.
St. Thomas', Strasbourg. *(Stoedtner)*
B.   *Claude Michel Clodion* (1738–1814). Satyr and Bacchante (*c.* 1775), terracotta. 23″ high. MMA, Bequest of Benjamin Altman, 1913.
C.   *Etienne-Maurice Falconet* (1716–1791). Venus Spanking Cupid, marble. 18½″ high. MFA.
D.   *Jones* (1573–1652). London, Banqueting House (1619–1621). 120′ long x 75′ high.
E.   *Jones.* Greenwich, Queen's House (1617–1635). 116′ x 116′ x 43′ high.
F.   *Pratt* (1620–1685). Coleshill, ceiling (1650–1662). 40′ x 22′. *(Stoedtner)*

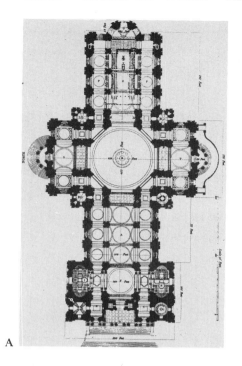

A

C

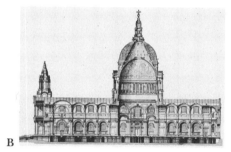

B

D

E

A. *Wren* (1632–1723). London, St. Paul's (1675–1710). 514' x 250'.
B. London, St. Paul's, longitudinal section. Total height, 366'. *(Stoedtner)*
C. London, St. Paul's, east end. (© TWA)
D. London, St. Paul's, west end.
E. London, St. Paul's, interior.

A

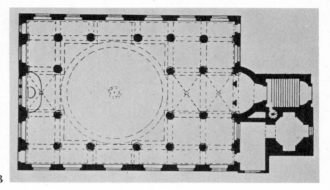

B

C

D

E

A.   *Wren* (1632–1723). London, City Plan (1666). *(Stoedtner)*
B.   *Wren*. London, St. Stephen's Walbrook (1672–1679). 82′ 6″ x 75′.
C.   *Wren*. London, St. Mary-le-Bow (1671–1683). Total height, 223′. *(BIS)*
D.   London, St. Stephen's Walbrook, interior. *(Stoedtner)*
E.   *Wren*. Greenwich, Royal Hospital (1676–1716). 150′ high. *(Stoedtner)*

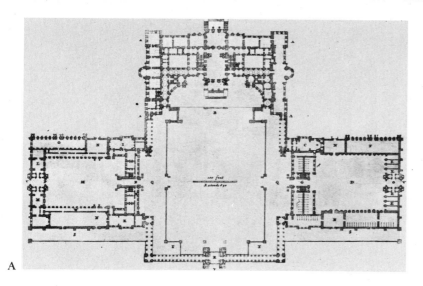

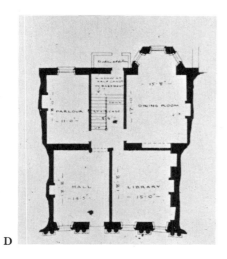

A.   *Vanbrugh* (1666–1726). Blenheim Castle (1705–1724). 870′ x 480′. *(Stoedtner)*
B.   Blenheim Castle, the Hall. *(Country Life)*
C.   Blenheim Castle, Court façade. *(Country Life)*
D.   *Wood* (*c.* 1704–1754). Bath, the Circus, house plans (1754). *c.* 35′ x 49′.
E.   *Wood.* Bath, Queen's Square. *c.* 200′ long. *(Stoedtner)*

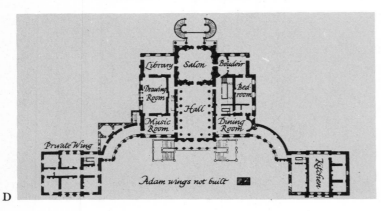

A. *Wood* (*c.* 1704–1754). Bath, Prior Park (1735–1743). 147′ long; columns, 32′ high. *(Stoedtner)*
B. *Gibbs* (1682–1754). London, St. Martin's in the Fields (1721–1726). 185′ high. *(Stoedtner)*
C. *Adam* (1728–1792). Kedleston, south front (1760–1768). 125′ wide.
D. Kedleston, plan. 360′ total width. (C. Hussy, *English Country Houses,* Country Life, Ltd.)
E. Kedleston, interior.

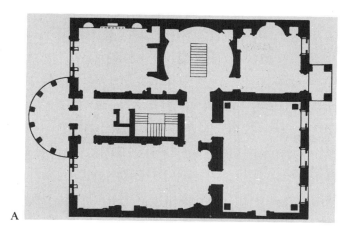

A. *Adam* (1728–1792). London, Home House (1775–1777). 60′ x 70′. EMU.
B. London, Home House, interior.
C. London, Home House, interior detail.
D. *Adam.* London, Kenwood, Library (1767). 60′ x 22′ x 24′ high. *(Stoedtner)*
E. *Unknown British painter* (*fl.* 1603). Henry Frederick, Prince of Wales, and Sir John Harington. 79½″ x 58″.
MMA, Joseph Pulitzer Fund, 1944.
F. *Sir Peter Lely* (1618–1680). Nell Gwynn (*c.* 1675). 47½″ x 38″. Nat. Portrait Gal., London. *(Mansell)*

A.   *William Hogarth* (1697–1764). The Artist's Servants. 24½″ x 29¼″. Nat. Gal., London. *(Stoedtner)*
B.   *William Hogarth.* Marriage à la Mode, Plate III (1745), engraving. MMA.
C.   *William Hogarth,* Calais Gate (1749). 31″ x 37¼″. Nat. Gal., London. *(Stoedtner)*
D.   *William Hogarth.* The Shrimp Girl (last period). 25″ x 20¾″. Nat. Gal., London. *(BIS)*
E.   *Thomas Rowlandson* (1756–1827). The Exhibition Starecase, etching. MMA, Elisha Whittelsey Coll., 1959.

A. *Joshua Reynolds* (1723–1792). Lord Heathfield. 56″ x 44¾″. Nat. Gal., London. *(Stoedtner)*
B. *Joshua Reynolds.* Dr. Johnson (1772–1780). 3′6″ x 2′1″. Nat. Gal., London. *(Stoedtner)*
C. *Henry Raeburn* (1756–1823). Captain Robert Hay of Spot. *c.* 7′10½″ x 4′11″. Louvre. *(Arch. Photo.)*
D. *Thomas Gainsborough* (1727–1788). Countess Anne Duncombe. Wertheimer, London. *(Stoedtner)*
E. *Thomas Gainsborough.* Robert Andrews and His Wife (*c.* 1748–1750). 27″ x 47″.
Coll. G. W. Andrews, Reelhill, Surrey, England. *(Mansell)*

A.   *Thomas Lawrence* (1769–1830). The Calmady Children. 30⅞″ x 30⅛″. MMA, Bequest of Collis P. Huntington, 1925.
B.   *Thomas Lawrence.* Sarah Moulton-Barrett: "Pinkie." 57½″ x 39¼″. Huntington Library, San Marino, Calif.
C.   *William Blake* (1757–1827). Illustration for the Book of Job (1825), engraving. 7¾″ x 5⅞″. Philadelphia Mus. Art, Gift of
Staunton B. Peck.
D.   *William Blake.* Whirlwind of Lovers, from Dante's *Divine Comedy,* 1827. 10⅞″ x 13⅞″. Nat. Gal., Wash., Leesing J. Rosenwald Coll.
E.   *Samuel Palmer* (1805–1881). Opening the Fold (1880), etching. 4⅝″ x 7″. Coll. Carl Zigrosser, Chestnut Hill, Pa.
F.   *Henry Fuseli* (1741–1825). Nightmare (*c.* 1780–1790). 40″ x 50″. Detroit Inst. Arts.

A. *Soane* (1753–1837). London, Bank of England, Lothbury Angle (1788–1835). Column height, 23′ 4″.
B. *Soane*. London, Soane Museum (1812–1813). 18′ 6″ wide.
C. London, Bank of England, Colonial Office, Barrel vaults, 22′ high. *(Natl. Bldgs. Record)*
D. *Vignon* (1762–1829). Paris, La Madeleine (1806–1842). 350′ x 147′.
E. Paris, La Madeleine, interior. *(Stoedtner)*

A

B

C

D

E

A. *Percier* and *Fontaine*. Paris, Arc du Carrousel (1807). 63½′ wide x 48′ high. *(FGTO)*
B. *Chalgrin* (1739–1811). Paris, Arc de Triomphe (1806–1836). 146′ x 72′ x 160′ high. *(FGTO)*
C. *Bianchi* (1787–1849). Naples, San Francesco di Paola (1816–1824). *(Alinari)*
D. *Langhans* (1733–1808). Berlin, Brandenburg Gate (1789–1793).
E. *Von Klenze* (1784–1864). Regensburg, Valhalla (1830–1842). *(Stoedtner)*

A. *Nash* (1752–1835). Brighton, Royal Pavilion (1815–1818). Center unit, 50′ wide. *(Nat. Bldgs. Record)*
B. *Wyatt* (1748–1813). Fonthill Abbey (1796–1813). 225′ high.
C. Fonthill Abbey, interior. *c.* 245′ long x 35′ wide.
D. *Barry* (1795–1860). London, House of Parliament (1840–1860). 940′ long. *(BIS)*
E. *Barry.* London, Traveller's Club (1829–1831). 75′ wide. *(Nat. Bldgs. Record)*
F. *Street* (1824–1881). London, Law Courts (1868–1882). *c.* 500′ long. *(Stoedtner)*

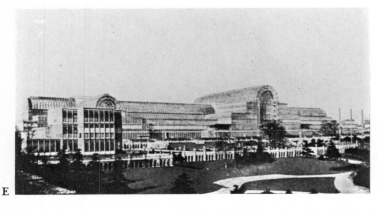

A.   *Gau* and *Ballu*. Paris, Sainte Clothilde (1846–1859). 105' wide x 216' high. *(Stoedtner)*
B.   *Labrouste* (1801–1875). Paris, Bibliothèque Sainte Geneviève (1843–1850). *c.* 336' long.
C.   Paris, Bibliothèque Sainte Geneviève, Reading Room. 330' x 66' x 42' high. *(Arch. Photo.)*
D.   *Brunel* and *Wyatt*. London, Paddington Station (1854).
E.   *Paxton* (1803–1865). London, Crystal Palace (1851). 1608' long.
F.   London, Crystal Palace, interior. *(Dickinson's Comprehensive Pictures of the Great Exhibition, London, 1854)*

A. *Garnier* (1825–1898). Paris, Opera House, façade (1861–1874). *c.* 200′ wide x 95′ high. *(FGTO)*
B. Paris, Opera House, stairway. *(FGTO)*
C. *Visconti* and *Lefuel*. Paris, Louvre, Pavilion Colbert (1852–1857). *(Giraudon)*
D. *Abadie* (1812–1884). Paris, Sacré Coeur (begun 1873). 328′ x 164′ x 264′ high. *(FGTO)*
E. *Saulnier*. Noisel-sur-Marne, Menier Chocolate Works (1871–1872). (S. Giedion, *Space, Time and Architecture*, Harvard Univ. Press)

A

B

C

D

E

A.   *Webb* (1830–1915). Bexley Heath, Red House (1859). *c.* 30′ high. (*Nat. Bldgs. Record*)
B.   *Shaw* (1831–1912). London, New Scotland Yard (1887).
C.   *Shaw*. London, Fred White House (1887). (*Nat. Bldgs. Record*)
D. *François Rude* (1784–1855). Departure of Volunteers of 1792 (1833–1836). *c.* 46′ x 42′. Arc de Triomphe, Paris. (*Arch. Photo.*)
E. *Jean Baptiste Carpeau* (1827–1875). The Dance (1867–1869). *c.* 15′ x 8′6″. Façade, L'Opéra, Paris. (*Arch. Photo.*)

A. *Antonio Canova* (1757–1822). Pauline Borghese as Venus. Life size. Borghese Gal., Rome. *(Stoedtner)*
B. *Honoré Daumier* (1808–1879). Ratapoil. *c.* 15″ high. Louvre. *(Arch. Photo.)*
C. *Antoine-Louis Barye* (1795–1875). Lion and Serpent. Tuileries. *(Arch. Photo.)*
D. *Constantin Emile Meunier* (1831–1905). Marteleur. Life size. Mus. du Luxembourg. *(Arch. Photo.)*
E. *Edgar Degas* (1834–1917). Dancer Looking at the Sole of Her Right Foot (1882–1895). 18″ high. MMA.

A. *Auguste Rodin* (1840–1917). Burghers of Calais. *c.* 77½″ high. Rodin Mus., Paris. *(Arch. Photo.)*
B. *Auguste Rodin.* Monument to Balzac (1897). 9′3″ high. MOMA, presented in memory of Curt Valentin by his friends.
C. *Jacques Louis David* (1748–1825). The Oath of Horatius (after 1784). 50″ x 65″. Toledo Mus. Art, Gift of Edward Drummond Libbey.
D. *Jacques Louis David.* Marat Assassinated (1793). 65″ x 50⅜″. Mus. Roy. des Beaux Arts, Brussels.
E. *Jacques Louis David.* M. Sériziat (1785). Panel 51½″ x 37¾″. Louvre.
F. *Jacques Louis David.* Sacre, or Coronation (1805). 240″ x 366½″. Louvre.

A. *Jacques Louis David* (1748–1825). Madame Récamier (1800). 68″ x 85¾″ Louvre.
B. *François Pascal Gérard* (1770–1837). Madame Récamier. *c.* 90½″ x 57″. Carnavalet, Paris. *(French Cult. Serv.)*
C. *Pierre-Paul Prud'hon* (1758–1823). Abduction of Psyche. Louvre. *c.* 76¹¹⁄₁₆″ x 61¹³⁄₁₆″. *(French Cult. Serv.)*
D. *Anne-Louise Girodet-Trioson* (1767–1824). Burial of Atala (1808). 82¾″ x 105″. Louvre.
E. *Antoine Jean Gros* (1771–1835). Napoleon Visiting the Pesthouse at Jaffa (1804). 209″ x 283″. Louvre.

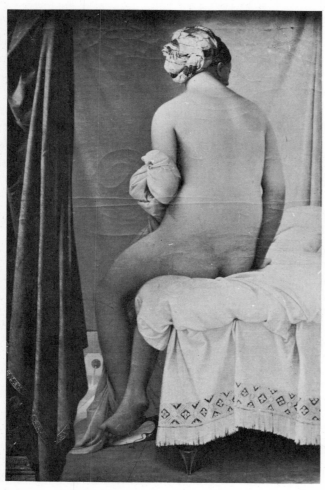

A.   *J. A. D. Ingres* (1780–1867). François Marius Granet. 28¾″ x 24″. Aix-en-Provence.
B.   *J. A. D. Ingres*. Roger and Angelica (1867). 15⅜″ x 18½″. Nat. Gal., London *(Arch. Photo.)*
C.   *J. A. D. Ingres*. Madame Rivière (Salon, 1806). Oval, 45⅝″ x 35½″. Louvre. *(Giraudon)*
D.   *J. A. D. Ingres*. Bather of Valpinçon (1808). 56⅝″ x 38¼″. Louvre. *(Giraudon)*

A

B

C

D

A.   *Théodore Géricault* (1791–1824). Raft of Medusa (1818). 193″ x 282″. Louvre.
B.   *Théodore Géricault.* Madwoman *c.* 30⅓″ x 25-2/5″. Louvre. *(Arch. Photo.)*
C.   *Ferdinand Eugène Delacroix* (1798–1863). Dante and Virgil in Hell (1821–1822). 73½″ x 94½″. Louvre.
D.   *Théodore Géricault.* After Death (*c.* 1818, a study). 17¾″ x 22″. Art Inst., Chicago, Munger Coll. (McKay Fund).

A.   *Théodore Géricault* (1791–1824). Wounded Cuirassier Leaving the Field (1814). *c.* 115″ x 89⅓″. Louvre. *(Arch. Photo.)*
B.   *Théodore Géricault*. Riderless Races at Rome (1817). 17″ x 23″. Walters Art. Gal., Baltimore.
C.   *Ferdinand Eugène Delacroix* (1798–1863). Arabian Horses Fighting in a Stable (1860). *c.* 26½″ x 32¼″. Louvre. *(Arch. Photo.)*
D.   *Ferdinand Eugène Delacroix*. Self-portrait (1837 or 1838). 25¼″ x 20″. Louvre.
E.   *Ferdinand Eugène Delacroix*. Roger Saving Angelique (1847). 11″ x 14″. Louvre. *(Arch. Photo.)*

A. *Eugène Delacroix* (1798–1863). Woman of Algiers (1834). *c.* 71″ x 90″. Louvre. *(French Cult. Serv.)*
B. *Eugène Delacroix*. The Massacre of Chios (1824). 13′10″ x 11′7″. Louvre. *(Arch. Photo.)*
C. *Eugène Delacroix*. The Abduction of Rebecca (1846). 39½″ x 32¼″. MMA, Wolfe Fund, 1903.
D. *Théodore Chassériau* (1819–1857). Peace (1844–1848), detail. *c.* 11′2″ x 11′10½″. Louvre. *(Arch. Photo.)*

A.   *Jean L. E. Meissonier* (1815–1891). "1814" (1864). 19¼" x 29½". Louvre.
B.   *Thomas Couture* (1815–1879). The Romans of the Decadence (1847). 181" x 304¼". Louvre.
C.   *Jean François Millet* (1814–1875). The Gleaners (1857). 33" x 44". Louvre.
D.   *Jean François Millet*. The Quarriers. 29" x 23½". Toledo Mus. Art, Gift of Arthur J. Secor.
E.   *Théodore Rousseau* (1812–1867). Under the Birches (1842). 16⅝" x 25⅜". Toledo Mus. Art, Gift of Arthur J. Secor.
F.   *Narcisse Diaz* (1807?–1876). Forest Path. 28" x 23¾". Philadelphia Mus. Art, John C. Johnson Coll.

A

B

C

D

A.   *Jean Baptiste Corot* (1796–1875). Self-portrait (1835). *c.* 13⅜″ x 9¹³⁄₁₆″. Uffizi. *(French Cult. Serv.)*
B.   *Jean Baptiste Corot*. Chartres Cathedral. 24⅜″ x 19¾″. Louvre. *(Arch. Photo.)*
C.   *Honoré Daumier* (1808–1879). Corot Sketching at Ville d'Avray (*c.* 1854–1856). 12½″ x 9½″. MMA, Bequest of Mrs. H. O. Havemeyer, The H. O. Havemeyer Coll.
D.   *Jean Baptiste Corot*. The Atelier. 24⅜″ x 16⅛″. Louvre. *(Arch. Photo.)*

A.   *Jean Baptiste Corot* (1796–1875). Bridge of Narni. 14⅛″ x 18½″. Louvre. (Arch. Photo.)

B.   *Jean Baptiste Corot.* Woman Gathering Faggots. 28⅜″ x 22½″. MMA, The Mr. and Mrs. Isaac D. Fletcher Coll., Bequest of Isaac D. Fletcher, 1917.

C.   *Charles François Daubigny* (1817–1878). Evening. 22¾″ x 36½″. MMA, Bequest of Robert Graham Dun, 1911.

D.   *Adolph Monticelli* (1824–1886). As You Like It. 17″ x 29″. Phillips Coll., Wash.

A

D

C

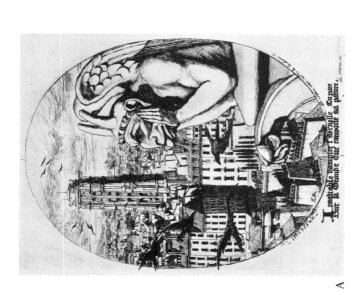

B

A. *Charles Meryon* (1821–1868). Le Stryge. MMA, Bequest of Mrs. H. O. Havemeyer, 1929, H. D. Havemeyer Coll.
B. *Honoré Daumier* (1808–1879). Rue Transnonain (1834), lithograph. c. 11½″ x 17½″. MMA, Rogers Fund, 1920.
C. *Honoré Daumier.* Crispin and Scapin. Louvre (1858–1860). c. 32⅜″ x 23⅜″. (*French Cult. Serv.*)
D. *Honoré Daumier.* The Witnesses (1872), lithograph. 10″ x 8¾″. MMA.

A.   *Honoré Daumier* (1808–1879). La Soupe, drawing. 11″ x 15¾″. Louvre.
B.   *Gustave Courbet* (1819–1877). Detail of Studio *(see below)*. Louvre. *(Arch. Photo.)*
C.   *Honoré Daumier.* The Artist at His Easel. 13⅛″ x 10¼″. Coll. Marjorie Phillips, Wash.
D.   *Gustave Courbet.* The Painter's Studio (1854–1855). 12′ x 18′. Louvre.

A. *Gustave Courbet* (1819–1877). Burial at Ornans (1849). 10' 3" x 21' 9". Louvre. *(Arch. Photo.)*
B. *Gustave Courbet.* La Toilette de la Mariée (1865–1870). 74" x 99". Mus. of Art, Smith College, Mass.
C. *Gustave Courbet.* The Wave (1870). 46" x 63". Louvre. *(Arch. Photo.)*

A

B

C

D

E

A.   *Constantine Guys* (1802–1892). Une Élégante (1850–1860), wash drawing. 15¼″ x 10½″. Fogg, Maurice Wertheim Coll.
B.   *Édouard Manet* (1832–1883). Déjeuner sur l'Herbe (1863). 84¼″ x 106¼″. Louvre.
C.   *Édouard Manet*. Alabama and Kearsarge (*c.* 1864). 54⅝″ x 51⅛″. John C. Johnson Coll., Philadelphia.
D.   *Édouard Manet*. Restaurant of Père Lathuille. Tournai. *(Stoedtner)*
E.   *Édouard Manet*. The Races at Longchamp (1864). 33¼″ x 17¼″. Art. Inst., Chicago, Potter Palmer Coll.

A

B

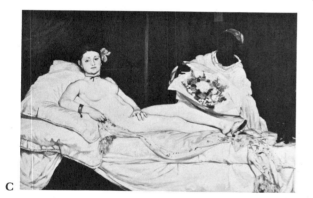

C

D

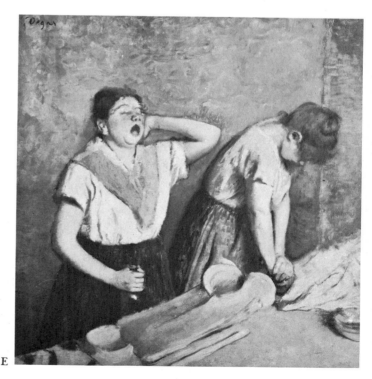

E

A.   *Édouard Manet* (1832–1883). Portrait of Zola (1868). 57½″ x 43¼″. Louvre.
B.   *Berthe Morisot* (1841–1895). In the Dining Room. 24¼″ x 19¾″. Nat. Gal., Wash., Chester Dale Coll.
C.   *Édouard Manet.* Olympia (1863). 51¼″ x 74¾″. Louvre.
D.   *Édouard Manet.* The Bar at the Folies Bergères (1881). 37¾″ x 50″. Coll. Courtauld, London.
E.   *Edgar Degas* (1834–1917). Woman Ironing (1882). 31″ x 28¾″. Durand-Ruel, Paris.

A. *Mary Cassatt* (1845–1926). La Toilette. 39″ x 26″. Art. Inst., Chicago, Robert Alexander Waller Mem. Coll.
B. *Edgar Degas* (1834–1917). Degas' Father Listening to Pagans (*c.* 1869–1872). 31½″ x 24¾″. MFA, John T. Spaulding Coll.
C. *Edgar Degas.* The Tub (1886). 26½″ x 26½″. Hill-Stead Mus., Farmington, Conn. *(Miller)*
D. *Edgar Degas.* At the Races: Amateur Jockeys near a Carriage (1887–1880). 26″ x 32½″. Louvre. *(Arch. Photo.)*
E. *Edgar Degas.* Cafe, Boulevard Montmartre (1877), pastel. 16½″ x 23½″. Louvre.

A. *Edgar Degas* (1834–1917). The Bellelli Family (1859). 78¾″ x 99½″. Louvre.
B. *Claude Monet* (1840–1926). Terrace at Le Havre (1866). 23½″ x 31½″. Rev. T. Pitcairn Coll., Bryn Athyn, Pa.
C. *Frédéric Bazille* (1841–1870). Family Gathering (1868; retouched 1869). 60¾″ x 91″. Louvre.
D. *Camille Pissarro* (1830–1903). Hillside at Jallais, Pontoise (1867). 34¼″ x 45¼″. MMA, Bequest of William Church Osborne, 1951.
E. *Frédéric Bazille*. The Artist's Studio (1870). 38⅞″ x 47″. Louvre.

A. *Alfred Sisley* (1839–1899). Flood at Port Marly in 1876 (1876). 23⅝″ x 31⅞″. *(Arch. Photo.)*
B. *Eugène Louis Boudin* (1825–1898). Approaching Storm (1864). 14⅜″ x 22¾″. Art. Inst., Chicago, Gift of Annie Swan Coburn to the Mr. and Mrs. Lewis L. Coburn Memorial.
C. *Claude Monet* (1840–1926). Old St. Lazare Station, Paris (1877). 23½″ x 31½″. Art. Inst., Chicago. *(French Cult. Serv.; Bulloz)*
D. *Claude Monet.* Rouen Cathedral (1894). 41½″ x 29″. MFA.
E. *Camille Pissarro* (1830–1903). Boulevard des Italiens, Morning Sunlight (1897). 28⅞″ x 36¼″. Nat. Gal., Wash., Chester Dale Coll.
F. *Claude Monet.* Water Lilies (c. 1920). 6′ 6½″ x 19′ 7½″. MOMA, Mrs. Simon Guggenheim Fund.

A

B

C

D

A. *Pierre Auguste Renoir* (1841–1919). Bal à Bougival (1883). 70¾″ x 38½″. MFA.
B. *Claude Monet* (1840–1926). Femme à l'Ombrelle (1886). *c.* 51-3/5″ x 34⅔″. Louvre. *(Arch. Photo.)*
C. *Pierre Auguste Renoir.* The Judgment of Paris (*c.* 1908–1910). 18⅝″ x 24⅛″. Phillips Coll.
D. *Pierre Auguste Renoir.* Bather (1884–1887). 20¼″ x 12″. Phila. Mus. Art, Louise and Walter Arensberg Coll.

A

B

C

D

E

F

A. *Claude Monet* (1840–1926). Le Basin d'Argenteuil. 21¾" x 29¼". Rhode Island School of Design, Provincetown.
B. *Georges Pierre Seurat* (1859–1891). Fishing Fleet at Port-en-Bessin (1888?). 21⅝" x 25⅝". Mus. Modern Art, New York.
Lillie P. Bliss Coll.
C. *Georges Pierre Seurat*. Bathing Party (1883–1884). 79" x 118½". Nat. Gal., London.
D. *Paul Signac* (1863–1935). View of the Port of Marseilles (1905). 35" x 45¾". MMA, Gift of Robert Lehman, 1955.
E. *Georges Pierre Seurat*. Parade (1889). 39½" x 59¼". MMA, Bequest of Stephen C. Clark, 1960.
F. *Georges Pierre Seurat*. A Sunday Afternoon on the Island of La Grande Jatte (1884–1886). 81¼" x 120¼". Art Inst., Chicago,
Helen Birch Bartlett Mem. Coll.

A

B

C

D

E

A.   *Paul Gauguin* (1848–1903). The Yellow Christ (1889). 36½″ x 29″. Albright Art Gal., Buffalo, N. Y. *(French Cult. Serv.)*
B.   *Georges Pierre Seurat* (1859–1891). Le Chahut (1889). 22″ x 18¼″. Albright Art Gal.
C.   *Paul Gauguin*. The Moon and the Earth (1893). 45″ x 24½″. MOMA, Lillie P. Bliss Coll.
D.   *Paul Gauguin*. Auti Te Pape, woodcut. MMA, Rogers Fund, 1921.
E.   *Henri de Toulouse-Lautrec* (1864–1901). La Goulue (1894), lithograph. 11-13/16″ x 9⅞″.
MOMA, Mrs. John D. Rockefeller, Jr., Fund.

A. *Henri de Toulouse-Lautrec* (1864–1901). The Jockey (Oct. 1899). *c.* 20″ x 14½″ *(French Cult. Serv.)*
    B. *Henri de Toulouse-Lautrec.* A La Mie (1891). *c.* 20″ x 28″. MFA.
C. *Vincent van Gogh* (1853–1890). Self-portrait (1888). 24½″ x 20½″. Fogg, Maurice Wertheim Coll.
    D. *Henri de Toulouse-Lautrec.* The Salon in the Rue des Moulins (1894). 43⅞″ x 52½″. Albi, France.
    E. *Vincent van Gogh.* Potato Eaters (1885). 32¼″ x 45″. Kröller Müller Mus., Otterlo, The Netherlands.

A. *Vincent van Gogh* (1853–1890). Night Café (1888). 28¾″ x 36¼″. Yale Univ. Art. Gal., Gift of Stephen C. Clark. *(MOMA)*
B. *Vincent van Gogh*. Cornfield with Cypress. 28½″ x 25¾″. Nat. Gal., London.
C. *Vincent van Gogh*. Sunflowers (1888). 36¼″ x 28⅞″. Coll. of Mrs. Carroll S. Tyson, Chestnut Hill, Pa.
D. *Vincent van Gogh*. Sunflowers. 24″ x 17″. MMA, Rogers Fund, 1949.
E. *Vincent van Gogh*. The Ravine (Dec. 1889). 28¾″ x 36¼″. MFA.

A. *Vincent van Gogh* (1853–1890). The Starry Night (1889). 29″ x 36¼″. MOMA, Lillie P. Bliss Bequest.
B. *Vincent van Gogh*. Portrait of Dr. Gachet (May 1890), an etching. 7⅛″ x 5¹⁵⁄₁₆″. MOMA, Gift of Mrs. John D. Rockefeller, Jr.
C. *Paul Cézanne* (1839–1906). Self-portrait. 24″ x 18½″. Phillips Coll.
D. *Paul Cézanne*. La Maison du Pendu, or The Suicide's House (1872–1873). 19⅞″ x 26¼″. Louvre. (*French Cult. Serv.*)

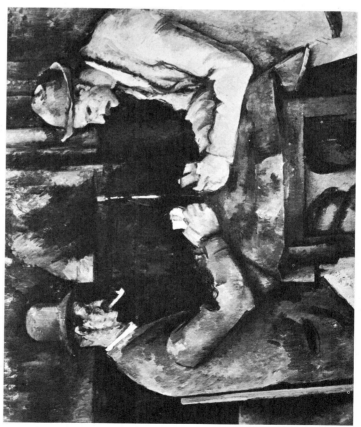

A. *Pierre Cécile Puvis de Chavannes (1824–1898). The Sacred Grove (after 1883).* 36½" x 6' 10⅞". Art. Inst., Chicago,
     Potter Palmer Coll.
B. *Paul Cézanne (1839–1906). Still Life (1895–1900).* 28¾" x 36¼". Louvre. *(Arch. Photo.)*
C. *Paul Cézanne. Two Card Players (c. 1892).* 17¾" x 22½". Louvre. *(Arch. Photo.)*
D. *Paul Cézanne. La Lutte d'Amour (1875–1876).* 15" x 18½". Mr. and Mrs. Averell Harriman Coll. *(Oliver Baker)*

A

B

C

D

A. *Paul Cézanne* (1839–1906). The Gulf of Marseilles Seen from L'Estaque. 28¾" x 39½". MMA, Bequest of Mrs. H. O. Havemeyer, 1929, H. O. Havemeyer Coll.
B. *Odilon Redon* (1840–1916). Vase of Flowers (1914). 28¾" x 21⅛". MOMA, Gift of William S. Paley.
C. *Paul Cézanne*. Mont Sainte-Victoire Seen from Bibemus Quarry (c. 1898–1900). 25½" x 32". Baltimore Mus. Art, Cone Coll.
D. *Odilon Redon*. The Wing (1893), lithograph. 12½" x 9⅝". MOMA, Lillie P. Bliss Coll. *(Oliver Baker)*

A. *Gustave Moreau* (1826–1898). The Apparition or The Dance of Salomé (*c.* 1876). 21¾″ x 17½″.
Fogg, Grenville L. Winthrop Bequest.
B. *Henri Rousseau* (1844–1910). The Snake Charmer (1907). 65″ x 73¼″. Louvre. *(Arch. Photo.)*
C. *Henri Rousseau.* Poet and His Muse. 57½″ x 38¼″. Kunstmus., Basel, Switzerland. *(Stoedtner)*
D. *Henri Rousseau.* The Sleeping Gypsy (1897). 51″ x 79″. MOMA, Gift of Mrs. Simon Guggenheim.

A

B

C

A. *Thomas Girtin* (1775–1802). Kirkstall Abbey. 12″ x 20⅞″. Victoria and Albert Mus.
B. *R. P. Bonington* (1802–1828). Gardens of Versailles. *c.* 16½″ x 20½″. Louvre. (*Arch. Photo.*)
C. *John Constable* (1776–1837). Study for the Leaping Horse. Victoria and Albert Mus.

A

B

C

D

A. *John Constable* (1776–1837). A Study for the Hay Wain. 50½″ x 73″. Victoria and Albert Mus.
B. *John Constable.* Study for the Valley Farm. 57½″ x 49″. Victoria and Albert Mus.
C. *John Constable.* The Hay Wain (1821). 50½″ x 73″. Nat. Gal., London.
D. *J. M. William Turner* (1775–1851). Dido Building Carthage (1815). 60½″ x 89½″. Nat. Gal., London.

A.   *J. M. William Turner* (1775–1851). Calais Pier (1802–1803). 67¾" x 94½". Nat. Gal., London. (*Mansell*)
B.   *J. M. William Turner.* Fighting Temeraire (1838–1839). 35½" x 47½". Nat. Gal., London.
C.   *J. M. William Turner.* Steamer in a Snowstorm (1842). 35½" x 47½". Nat. Gal., London.
D.   *J. M. William Turner.* Cottage Destroyed by an Avalanche. Tate Gal., London. (*Mansell*)

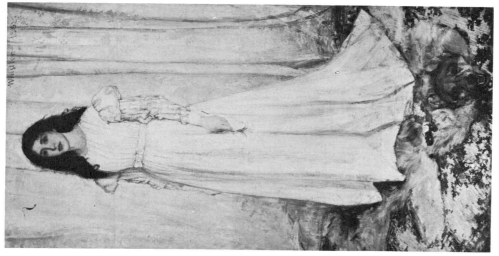

A. *Aubrey V. Beardsley* (1872–1898). "The Mysterious Rose Garden," from *The Yellow Book*, Vol. IV, January 1895.
B. *William H. Hunt* (1790–1864). The Awakening Conscience (1855). 29¾" x 21⅝". Sir Colin Anderson Coll., London.
C. *Dante Gabriel Rossetti* (1828–1882). The Annunciation (1850). Tate Gal., London. (*Mansell*)
D. *James A. McNeill Whistler* (1834–1903). Black Lion Wharf, etching, IBM Corp.
E. *James A. McNeill Whistler.* The White Girl (1862). 85½" x 43". National Gallery of Art, Washington, D.C., Harris Whittemore Coll.

B

C

A

D

A. C. D. Friedrich (1774–1840). Cloister Graveyard in the Snow (1810). Panel, 47⅝" x 70". Nationalgal., Berlin (now lost).
B. James A. McNeill Whistler (1834–1903). Carlyle (1874). 67" x 56". Glasgow Art Gal. (Mansell)
C. Arnold Böcklin (1827–1901). The Isle of the Dead (1880). Panel, 29" x 48". MMA; Reisinger Fund, 1926.
D. Franz von Lenbach (1836–1904). Portrait of Richard Wagner. Private collection. (Stoedtner)

A. *Ferdinand Hodler* (1853–1918). Retreat at Marignano. Zurich. *(Stoedtner)*
B. *Adolph von Menzel* (1815–1905). The Balcony Room (1845). Ehem. Staat. Mus., Nat. Gal., (West) Berlin. *(Bruckmann)*
C. *Wilhelm Leibl* (1844–1900). Peasant Women in Church (1878–1882). Kunsthalle, Hamburg. *(Stoedtner)*
D. *Gaudi* (1852–1926). Barcelona, Sagrada Familia (begun 1903). Spires, 330′ high. *(Stoedtner)*
E. *Guimard* (1867–1942). Paris, Place de l'Etoile, Metro Station (*c.* 1900). *(Stoedtner)*
F. *Horta* (1861–1947). Brussels, Tassel House (1893).
G. *Hankar* (1861–1901). Brussels, Janssen's House. *(Stoedtner)*

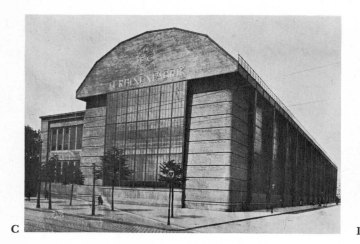

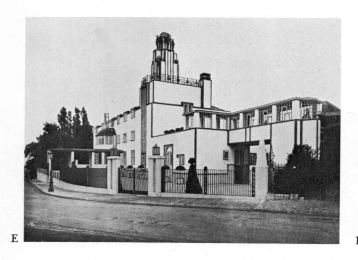

A. *Lutyens* (1869–1944). Sonning, Deanery Gardens (1901). 74′ wide. *(Country Life)*
B. *Lutyens.* Godalming, The Orchards (1898). Wing, 55′ wide. *(Stoedtner)*
C. *Behrens* (1868–1938). Berlin, A. E. G. Turbine Factory (1909). *(Stoedtner)*
D. *Wagner* (1841–1918). Vienna, Postal Savings Bank (1905). *(Stoedtner)*
E. *Hoffman* (1870–1956). Brussels, Stoclet House (1905–1911). 167′ wide. *(Stoedtner)*
F. *Bonatz* and *Scholer*. Stuttgart, Railroad Station (1911–1927). 630′ wide. *(Stoedtner)*

A. *Perret* (1874–1954). Le Raincy, Notre Dame (1922–1923). 66′ x 188′. *(Stoedtner)*
B. Le Raincy, Notre Dame. *(Stoedtner)*
C. *Jensen Klint* (1853–1930). Copenhagen, Gruntvig Church (1913–1926). 79′ wide. *(DIS)*
D. *Bartning* (1885–   ). Cologne, Steel Church (1928). *(Stoedtner)*
E. *Böhm* (1880–1955). Bischofsheim, Concrete Church (1926). *(Stoedtner)*
F. *Freyssinet* (1879–   ). Orly, Hangar (1916). Interior heights, 164′. *(Stoedtner)*

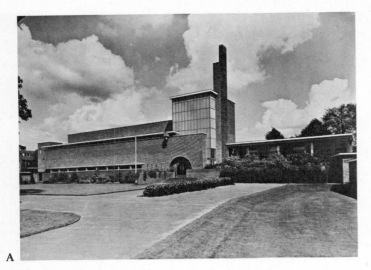

A. *Dudok* (1884–   ). Hilversum, High School (1921). *(NIS)*
B. *Hoeger* (1877–1949). Hamburg, Chile House (1923). 492′ long. *(Stoedtner)*
C. *Mendelssohn* (1887–1953). Stuttgart, Schocken Store (1926–1928). *(Stoedtner)*
D. *Mendelssohn.* Potsdam, Einstein Tower (1920–1921). *(Stoedtner)*
E. *Oud* (1890–   ). Hook of Holland. Workers' Houses (1924–1927). Housing units, 21′ wide. *(NIS)*
F. *Maillart* (1872–1940). Schwandbach Bridge (1933). (S. Giedion, *Space, Time, and Architecture*,
Harvard Univ. Press, 1941, 1954, 1959)

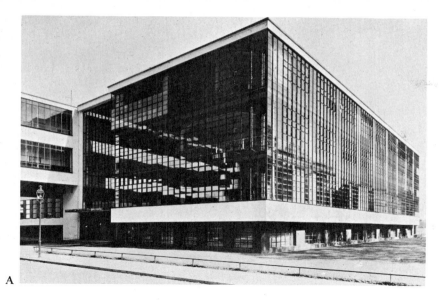

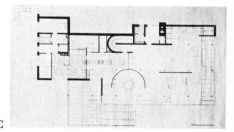

A.   *Gropius* (1883–   ). Dessau, Bauhaus (1925–1926). Main Block, 167′ x 49′.
B.   *Mies van der Rohe* (1886–   ). Barcelona, German Pavilion (1929). *(Stoedtner)*
C.   *Mies van der Rohe*. Brno, Tugendhat House (1930–1931). 115′ x 53′. *(Stoedtner)*
D.   Brno, Tugendhat House, street front.
E.   Brno, Tugendhat House, interior.
F.   Brno, Tugendhat House, view from rear.

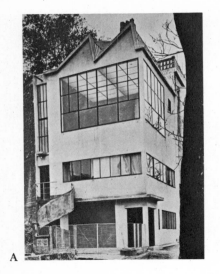

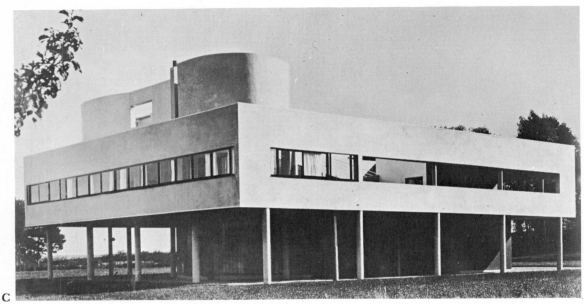

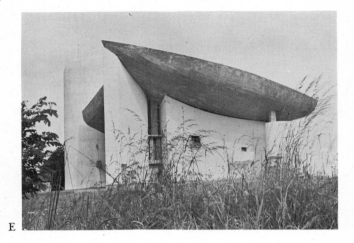

A.   *Le Corbusier* (1888–   ). Paris, Ozenfant House (1923). *(Stoedtner)*
B.   *Le Corbusier*. Garches, Stein House (1927). *c.* 60′ wide.
C.   *Le Corbusier*. Poissy-sur-Seine, Savoye House (1929–1930). 66′ x 74′ x 33′ high. *(MOMA)*
D.   *Le Corbusier*. Marseilles, Apartments. *(FGTO)*
E.   *Le Corbusier*. Ronchamps, Notre Dame du Haut (1950–1955). Tower, 72′ high. *(Lucien Hervé)*

A. *Montuori* and *Callini*. Rome, Termini Station (1947). *(ISTO)*

B. *Matthew* and *Martin*. London, Royal Festival Hall (1951). *c.* 240′ wide. *(ISTO;* T. Dannatt, ed., *Architects' Year Book,* 1960)

C. *Nervi* (1891–   ). Rome, Sports Palace (1959–1960). 300′ diameter. *(Courtesy of the architect)*

D. *Pierre Auguste Renoir* (1841–1919). The Judgment of Paris (1913–1916). 29¼″ high; 35½″ wide; 6¾″ deep. Cleveland Mus. Art, Mildred H. Lamb Coll., Purchase J. H. Wade Fund.

E. *Charles Despiau* (1874–1946). Assia (1938). 72¾″ high. MOMA, Gift of Mrs. Simon Guggenheim.

A.   *Aristide Maillol* (1861–1944). Chained Action (*c.* 1906). 47″ high. MMA (extended loan to MOMA).
B.   *Aristide Maillol.* Desire (c. 1904). 46⅞″ x 45″. MOMA, Gift of the sculptor.
C.   *Henri Matisse* (1869–1954). Reclining Nude I (1907). 13½″ high. Baltimore Mus. Art, Cone Coll.
D.   *Henri Matisse.* The Slave (1900–1903). 36¼″ high. Baltimore Mus. Art, Cone Coll.

A

B

C

D

A. *Marino Marini* (1901–   ). Horse and Rider (1947–1948). 38¼″ high. MOMA, Lillie P. Bliss Bequest.
B. *Pablo Picasso* (1881–   ). Shepherd Holding Lamb. *c.* 86⅝″ high. R. S. Ingersoll Coll., Penllyn, Pa. *(Adolph Studly)*
C. *Ernst Barlach* (1870–1938). Man Drawing Sword (1911). 29½″ high. The Galleries of the Cranbrook Acad. Art, Bloomfield Hills, Mich.
D. *Wilhelm Lehmbruck* (1881–1919). Kneeling Woman (1911). 69½″ high. MOMA, Mrs. John D. Rockefeller, Jr., Fund.

A

B

C

D

E

A. *Pablo Picasso* (1881–   ). Head of a Woman (1909). 21⅛″ high. MOMA, Benjamin and David Scharps Fund.
B. *Alberto Giacometti* (1901–   ). Chariot (1950). 57″ high. MOMA.
C. *Umberto Boccioni* (1882–1916). Unique Forms of Continuity in Space (1913). 43½″ high. MOMA, Lillie P. Bliss Bequest.
D. *Méret Oppenheim* (1913–   ). Object—Fur-Covered Cup, Plate, and Spoon (1936). MOMA.
E. *Gerhard Marcks* (1889–   ). The Runners (1924). 7″ high. MOMA, Gift of Mrs. John D. Rockefeller, Jr.

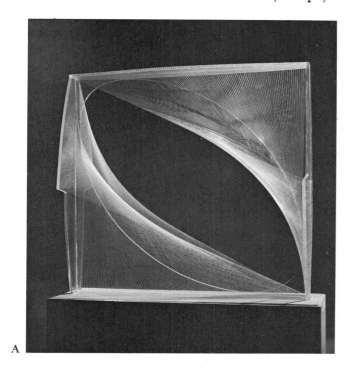

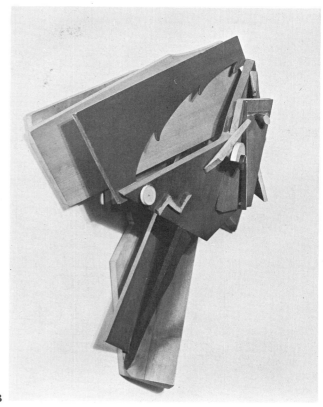

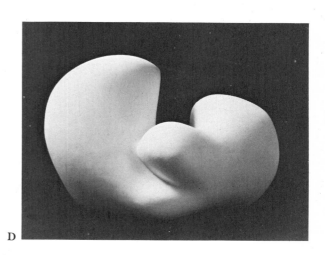

A. *Naum Gabo* (1890–   ). Linear Construction, Variation (1942–1943). 24¼″ high; 24¼″ long; 9¾″ wide at widest point. Phillips Coll.
B. *Henry Laurens* (1885–1954). Head (1918), wood construction. 20″ high. MOMA, van Gogh Purchase Fund.
C. *Raymond Duchamp-Villon* (1876–1918). The Horse (1914). 40″ high. MOMA, van Gogh Purchase Fund.
D. *Jean Arp* (1888–   ). Human Concretion (1935). 19½″ high. MOMA, Gift of Advisory Committee.

A

B

C

A.   *Constantin Brancusi* (1876-1957). Brancusi Sculpture. MOMA.
B.   *Henry Moore* (1898–   ). Reclining Figure (1935). 19″ high, 35″ long, 17¼″ wide. Albright Art. Gal.
C.   *Henry Moore.* The Bride (1940), cast head and copper wire. 9⅜″ high. MOMA, Lillie P. Bliss Coll.

A. *Edvard Munch* (1863–1944). Landscape by Night (1900). *c.* 31½" x 47". Kunsthaus, Zurich.
B. *Edvard Munch.* Anxiety (1896), color litho. 16¼" x 15¼". MOMA.
C. *Edvard Munch.* Girls on a Bridge. Nasjonalgal., Oslo.
D. *Edvard Munch.* The Kiss (1902), woodcut. 18¼" x 18¼". MOMA, Gift of Mrs. John D. Rockefeller, Jr.
E. *James Ensor* (1860–1949). The Cathedral (1886), etching. (*Stoedtner*)

A. *James Ensor* (1860–1949). Portrait of the Artist Surrounded by Masks (1889). 47½" x 31½". Cleomire Jussiant Coll., Antwerp. *(MOMA)*
B. *Emil Nolde* (1867–1956). Masks (1911). 28¾" x 30½". Nelson Gal., Friends of Art Coll.
C. *Georges Rouault* (1871–1958). Three Judges (1913). 29⅞" x 41⅝". MOMA, Sam A. Lewisholm Coll.
D. *Georges Rouault.* The Old King (1916–1936). 30¼" x 21¼". Carnegie Inst., Pittsburgh.

B

D

A

C

A. Edouard Vuillard (1868–1940). Mother and Sister of the Artist (c. 1893). 18¼" x 22¼". MOMA, Gift of Mrs. Saidie A. May.
B. Albert Marquet (1875–1947). Docks at Hamburg (1909). 27¼" x 32". Mme. Albert Marquet Coll., Bordeaux. (D. Stammirovitch)
C. Raoul Dufy (1877–1953). Anglers at Sunset (c. 1907). 21⅜" x 25⅝". MOMA, Gift of Mr. and Mrs. Charles Zadok.
D. Henri Matisse (1869–1954). Joy of Life (1905–1906). 68½" x 93¾". Barnes Found. Coll., Merion, Pa.

A.   *Henri Matisse* (1869–1954). Madame Matisse (1905). 16″ x 12¾″. Stat. Mus. Forkunst, Copenhagen.
B.   *Henri Matisse*. The Red Studio (1911). 71¼″ x 86¼″. MOMA, Mrs. Simon Guggenheim Fund.
C.   *Henri Matisse*. The Morrocans (1916). 71⅜″ x 110″. MOMA, Gift of Mr. and Mrs. Samuel A. Marx.
D.   *Henri Matisse*. Odalisque with Raised Arms. 25⅝″ x 19¾″. Nat. Gal., Wash.

A.   *Pablo Picasso* (1881–   ). The Old Guitarist (1903). 48″ x 37⅜″. Art. Inst., Chicago, Helen Birch Bartlett Mem. Coll.
B.   *Pablo Picasso.* Les Demoiselles d'Avignon (1907). 8′ x 7′8″. MOMA, Lillie P. Bliss Bequest.
C.   *Pablo Picasso.* Gertrude Stein (1906). 39⅜″ x 32″. MMA, Bequest of Gertrude Stein, 1946.
D.   *Pablo Picasso.* Man with Violin (1911). 39½″ x 28⅞″. Phila. Mus. Art, Louise and Walter Arensberg Coll.

A

B

C

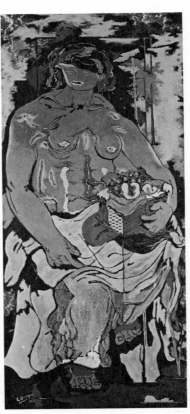

D

A. *Juan Gris* (1887–1927). Guitar and Flowers (1912). 44⅛″ x 27⅝″. MOMA, Bequest of Anna Erickson Levene in memory of her
husband, Dr. Phoebus Levene.
B. *Juan Gris.* Pierrot (1919). *c.* 35⁷⁄₁₆″ x 27½″. Mus. Nat. d'Art Moderne, Paris. *(Arch. Photo.)*
C. *Georges Braque* (1882–1963). Violin (1910). *c.* 46″ x 29″. Basel.
D. *Georges Braque.* Nude Woman with Basket of Fruit. 63¾″ x 29¼″. Nat. Gal., Wash., Chester Dale Coll.

A. *Robert Delaunay* (1885–1941). The Eiffel Tower (1914). 49½″ x 36″. Guggenheim Mus., N. Y.
B. *Roger de la Fresnaye* (1885–1925). The Conquest of the Air (1913). 7′ 8⅝″ x 6′ 5″. MOMA, Mrs. Simon Guggenheim Fund.
C. *Marcel Duchamp* (1887–1963). Nude Descending a Staircase—No. 2 (1912). 58″ x 35″. Phila. Mus. Art, Arensberg Coll.
D. *Kurt Schwitters* (1887–1948). Picture with Light Center (1919). 33¼″ x 25⅞″. MOMA.

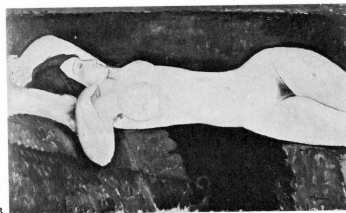

A. *Amedeo Modigliani* (1884–1920). Woman with Necklace (1917). 36″ x 23⅞″. Art Inst., Chicago, Charles H. and Mary F. S. Worcester Coll.

B. *Amedeo Modigliani.* Reclining Nude (*c.* 1919). 28½″ x 45⅞″. MOMA, Mrs. Simon Guggenheim Fund.

C. *Giorgio di Chirico* (1888–   ). Melancholy and Mystery of a Street (1914). 34⅜″ x 28¼″. Mr. and Mrs. Stanley Resor Coll., New Haven, Conn.

D. *Giacomo Balla* (1874–   ). Dog on Leash (1912). 35⅝″ x 43¼″. MOMA, A. Conger Goodyear Coll.

E. *Giorgio Morandi* (1890–   ). Still Life (1948). 16″ x 16″. Mr. and Mrs. Leo Lionni Coll., New York.

A. *Pablo Picasso* (1881–   ). Dog and Cock (1921). 60⅞″ x 30⅛″. Yale Univ. Art Gal., Gift of Stephen C. Clark.
B. *Pablo Picasso*. Girl before a Mirror (March, 1932). 63¾″ x 51¼″. MOMA, Gift of Mrs. Simon Guggenheim.
C. *Pablo Picasso*. Guernica (1937). 11′ 6″ x 25′ 8″. Extended loan to MOMA from the artist, M. Picasso.

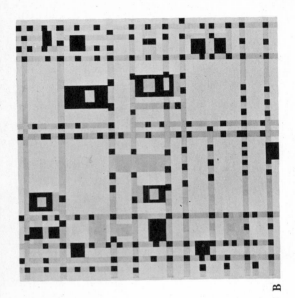

B

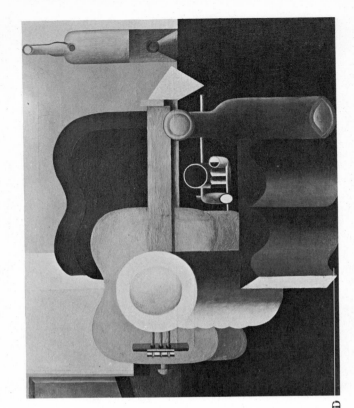

D

A

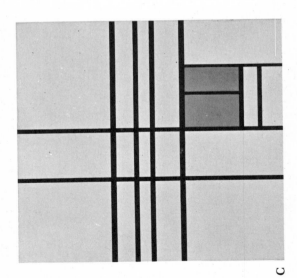

C

A.　*Piet Mondrian* (1872–1944). Horizontal Tree (1911). 29⅝″ x 43⅞″. Munson-Williams-Proctor Inst. Coll., Utica, N. Y.
　　B.　*Piet Mondrian.* Broadway Boogie Woogie (1942–1943). 50″ x 50″. MOMA.
C.　*Piet Mondrian.* Composition with Yellow (1936). 28¾″ x 26″. Phila. Mus. Art, Louise and Walter Arensberg Coll.
　　D.　*Le Corbusier* (1887–　　). Still Life (1920). 31⅞″ x 39¼″. MOMA, van Gogh Purchase Fund.

A. *Fernand Léger* (1881–1955). The City (1919). 91" x 116½". Phila. Mus. Art, Gallatin Coll.
B. *Marcel Gromaire* (1892–   ). Le Chemineau (1925). Emanuel Hoffmann Stiftung. (*Offent. Kunsts., Basel*)
C. *Joan Miró* (1893–   ). Dog Barking at the Moon (1926). 28¾" x 36¼". Phila. Mus. Art, A. E. Gallatin Coll.
D. *Joan Miró.* Composition (1933). 68½" x 77¼". MOMA, Gift of the Advisory Committee (by exchange).

A

B

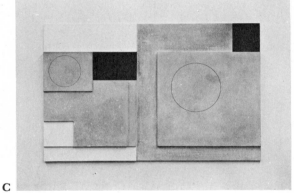

C

D

E

A. *Pierre Bonnard* (1867–1947). The Breakfast Room (*c.* 1930–1931). 63¼″ x 44⅛″. MOMA.
B. *Jules Pascin* (1885–1930). Salomé. Mus. d'Art Moderne, Paris. (*Arch. Photo.*)
C. *Ben Nicholson* (1894–   ). Relief (1939); Synthetic material, painted. 32⅞″ x 45″. MOMA, Gift of H. S. Ede and the artist.
D. *Chaim Soutine* (1894–1943). Windy Day, Auxerre (1939). 19½″ x 25⅝″. Phillips Coll.
E. *Graham Sutherland* (1903–   ). Horned Forms (1944). 39¼″ x 31⅞″. MOMA, Lillie P. Bliss Bequest.

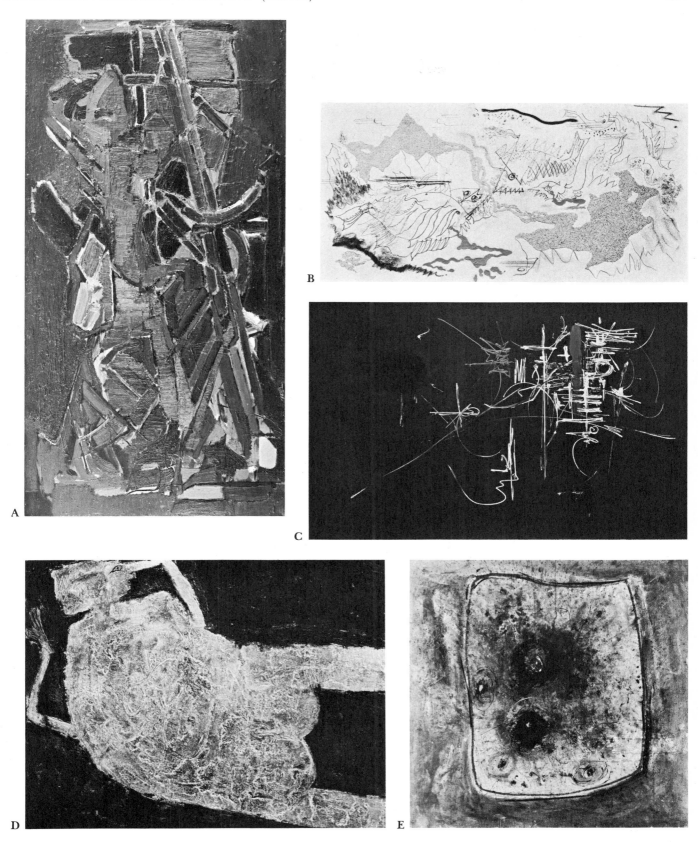

A.   *Nicholas de Stael* (1914–1955). Painting (1947). 77″ x 38⅜″. MOMA, Gift of Mr. and Mrs. Lee A. Ault.
B.   *André Masson* (1896–   ). Battle of Fishes (1927). 14¼″ x 28¾″. MOMA.
C.   *Georges Mathieu* (1921–   ). Painting (1952). 78¾″ x 118″. Guggenheim Mus.
D.   *Jean Dubuffet* (1904–   ). Nude Olympia (1950). 35″ x 45¾″. Larry Aldrich, New York.
E.   *Wols*, or *Alfred Otto Wolfgang Schulz* (1915–1951). Painting (1944–1945). 31⅞″ x 32″. MOMA, Mr. and Mrs. John de Menil Fund.

A.   *Ludwig Meidner* (1884–   ). Burning City. 26½″ x 31¼″ (double-faced). Morton D. May Collection. St Louis.
B.   *Käthe Kollwitz* (1867–1945). Death and the Mother (1934). 20⅛″ x 14⅜″.
C.   *Emil Nolde* (1867–1956). Life of Maria Aegyptiaca: First Episode, "Early Sinful Life" (1912). 33¼″ x 39¼″. Kunsthalle, Hamburg.
D.   *Karl Schmidt Rottluff* (1884–   ). The Three Kings (1917), woodcut. 19-9/16″ x 15⅜″. MOMA.
E.   *Franz Marc* (1880–1916). Blue Horses (*c.* 1911). 41¼″ x 71½″. Walker Art Cent., Minneapolis.
F.   *Max Beckmann* (1884–1950). The Night (1918–1919). 53″ x 60″. Berlin.

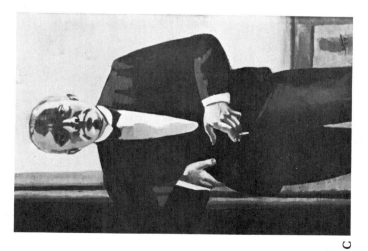

A. *Erich Heckel* (1883–   ). Convalescence of a Woman (1913), triptych. 32″ x 84″. Bush-Reisinger Mus., Cambridge, Mass.
B. *Ernst L. Kirchner* (1880–1938). The Street (1913). 47½″ x 35⅞″. MOMA.
C. *Max Beckmann* (1884–1950). Self-portrait in a Tuxedo (1927). 54½″ x 37¾″. Busch-Reisinger Mus.
D. *Max Beckmann.* Departure (1932–1935), triptych. Center panel, 84¾″ x 45⅜″; side panels, 84¾″ x 39¼″. MOMA.

A

B

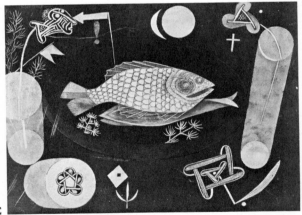

C

D

A.   *Oskar Kokoschka* (1886–   ). The Tempest, or The Wind's Bride (1914). Panel, 40¼″ x 75¼″. Kunstmus., Basel.
B.   *Paul Klee* (1879–1940). Twittering Machine (1922). 16¼″ x 12″. MOMA.
C.   *Paul Klee.* Around the Fish (1926). 18⅜″ x 25⅛″. MOMA, Mrs. John D. Rockefeller, Jr., Fund.
D.   *Kasimir Malevich* (1878–1935). Suprematist Composition, after pencil drawing of 1914–1915. 31⅝″ x 31⅝″. MOMA.

A.   *Marc Chagall* (1887–   ). Birthday (1915–1923). 31⅞″ x 39⅜″. Solomon R. Guggenheim Mus. Coll.
B.   *Vasily Kandinsky* (1866–1944). Composition No. 2 (1910). 38⅜″ x 51¾″ Solomon R. Guggenheim Mus. Coll.
C.   *Marc Chagall.* Bouquet with Flying Lovers (*c.* 1934–1937). 51⅜″ x 38⅜″. Tate Gal., London; © A.D.A.G.P., Paris.
D.   *Vasily Kandinsky.* Watercolor Abstraction (1910). *c.* 19¼″ x 25½″. (*M. DuMont Schauberg Buchverlag*)

A

B

C

D

E

F

G

A.   Mexico City, Cathedral (begun 1563). 145′ wide. (Kimball and Edgell, *Hist. of Arch.*, Harper)
B.   *Guerrero y Torres.* Guadalupe, Capilla del Pocito (1779). *(Arch Foto)*
C.   Santa Fe, Governor's Palace (1609). 400′ long. *(New Mexico State Tour. Bur.)*
D.   San Antonio, San José (1768).
E.   Tucson (near), San Xavier del Bac (1772–1797). 66′ wide.
F.   San Juan Capistrano, Mission (1797–1806). 30′ wide. EMU.
G.   Santa Barbara, Mission (1815–1920). *c.* 80′ wide. EMU.

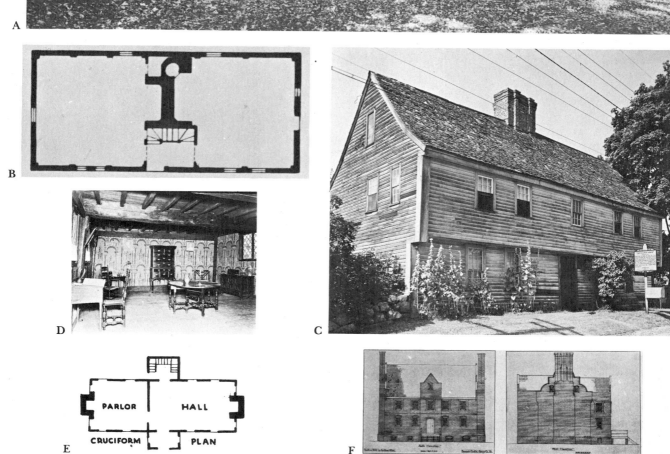

A.   Topsfield, Parson Capen House. *(Wayne Andrews)*
B.   Topsfield, Parson Capen House (1683). 42′ x 21′. EMU.
C.   Saugus, Scotch House (so called) (1651). 40′ wide x 26′ high. *(Wayne Andrews)*
D.   Boston, Paul Revere House.
E.   Virginia, Bacon's Castle (before 1676), plan. *c.* 48′ x 40′. (D. M. Mendelowitz, *A History of American Art*, p. 80)
F.   Bacon's Castle, restored. (Kimball, *Domestic Architecture of the American Colonies and Early Republic*, Scribner, 1922)

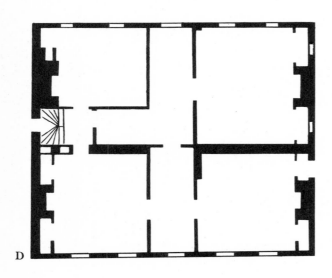

A.   Smithfield, St. Luke's (1632). *(Lib. Congress, Wash., D.C.)*
B.   Hingham, Old Ship Meeting House (1681). 55′ x 45′.
C.   Westover (1726). 63′ wide. *(Lib. Congress)*
D.   Medford, Royall House (1747). 45′ x 36′. EMU.
E.   Medford, Royall House, west front.

A.   Medford, Royall House, interior. *(George M. Cushing, Jr.)*
B.   Medford, Royall House, stair hall. *(George M. Cushing, Jr.)*
C.   Charleston, Brewton House (1765). Portico, *c.* 28' wide. *(Wayne Andrews)*
D.   New York, Jumel House (1765). Portico, *c.* 33' wide. EMU.
E.   Philadelphia, Independence Hall (1732–1752). *c.* 105' wide. *(Philadelphia Chamber of Commerce)*
F.   *Harrison* (1716–1775). Newport, Redwood Library (1748–1750). Portico, *c.* 26' wide. *(Wayne Andrews)*

A

B

C

D

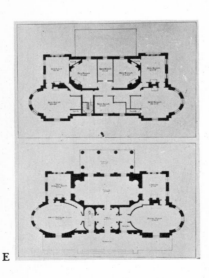

E

F

A.   Williamsburg, Bruton Church (1711–1715). 125′ long x 97′ high. *(Colonial Williamsburg Photo)*
B.   New York, St. Paul's Chapel (1764–1766). 140′ long. *(Wayne Andrews)*
C.   New York, St. Paul's Chapel. 66′ wide x 42′ high. *(Wayne Andrews)*
D.   Mount Vernon, river front (portico added 1786–1787). Portico, *c.* 100′ wide. *(Photo Abbie Rowe, NPS)*
E.   Philadelphia, Woodlands (remodeled 1788). *(Drawing by Ogden Codman)*
F.   Philadelphia, Woodlands. Portico, 37′ wide. *(Wayne Andrews)*

A. *Hoban* (*c.* 1762–1831). Washington, White House, north front (1792–1829). 168′ long x 50′ high. *(NPS)*
B. Washington, White House, south front. *(NPS)*
C. *McIntire* (1757–1811). Salem, Pierce Nichols House (1801). 9′ 2″ high.
D. *McComb* and *Mangin*. New York, City Hall (1803–1812). 215′ wide. *(Wayne Andrews)*
E. *Bulfinch* (1763–1844). Boston, State House (1795). 172′ x 65′ x 155′ high. *(Lib. Congress)*

A.   *Jefferson* (1743–1826). Richmond, State Capitol (1785–1798). 84' x 146' x 53' high. *(Richmond Chamber of Commerce)*
B.   *Jefferson.* Charlottesville, Monticello (1796–1808). 43' high. *(Virginia Chamber of Commerce)*
C.   *Jefferson.* Charlottesville, University of Virginia, Library (1817–1826). 77' diameter. *(Wayne Andrews)*
D.   *Latrobe* (1766–1820). Baltimore, Cathedral (1805–1821). Portico, *c.* 64' wide. *(Wayne Andrews)*
E.   *Latrobe, Bullfinch,* and *Walter.* Washington, Capitol. 280' high. *(Lib. Congress)*

A. *Hadfield* (1767–1826). Arlington, Lee Mansion (1826). Portico, 60′ wide. *(Wayne Andrews)*
B. *Town* and *Davis*. New York, Sub Treasury (1834–1841). Portico, 90′ wide. *(Lib. Congress)*
C. *Mills* (1781–1855). Washington, Monument (1836–1877). 555′ high. *(Stoedtner)*
D. *Renwick* (1818–1895). New York, St. Patrick's Cathedral (1850–1879). 328′ high. *(Stoedtner)*
E. *Upjohn* (1802–1878). New York, Trinity Church (1839–1846). 136′ x 72′ x 264′ high. EMU.

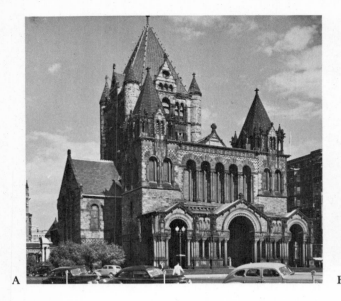

A.   *Richardson* (1838–1886). Boston, Trinity Church (1872–1877). 160′ x 121′ x 150′ high. *(Wayne Andrews)*
B.   *Richardson*. Chicago, Marshall Field Warehouse (1885–1887). 325′ x 190′ x 125′ high. *(MOMA)*
C.   *Roebling*. New York, Brooklyn Bridge (1870–1883). 1595′ long. *(Stoedtner)*
D.   *McKim, Mead,* and *White*. Boston, Public Library (1888–1895). 223′ x 226′ x 89′ high.
E.   *McKim, Mead,* and *White*. Chicago, World's Columbian Exposition, Agriculture Building (1893). 800′ long. *(Avery Lib.)*
F.   *Sullivan* (1856–1924). Chicago, World's Columbian Exposition, Transportation Building, door (1893). *(Chicago Hist. Soc.)*

A

B

C

D

E

A. *Buffington* (1847–1931). Cloudscraper Project (1887–1888).
B. *Burnham* and *Root*. Chicago, Monadnock Building (1891). 215' high.
C. *Burnham* and *Root*. Chicago, Masonic Temple (1892). 254' high. *(Stoedtner)*
D. *Sullivan* (1856–1924). St. Louis, Wainwright Building (1890–1891). 127' x 114' x 135' high. *(MOMA)*
E. *Sullivan*. Chicago, Schlessinger-Mayer Building (1899–1904). *c.* 265' x 150'. *(Chicago Arch. Photo.)*

A. *Gilbert* (1859–1934). New York, Woolworth Building (1913). 792' high. *(Wurts Bros.)*
B. *Saarinen* (1873–1950). Chicago, Tribune Tower Competition, second prize (1922). *(Kaufmann and Fabry)*
C. *McKenzie, Voorhees,* and *Gmelin.* New York, Barclay-Vesey Telephone Building (1924–1926). 498' high. *(Jack Steinberg)*
D. *Corbett* and others. New York, R.C.A. Building (1933). 850' high. *(Stoedtner)*
E. *Skidmore, Owings,* and *Merrill.* New York, Lever House (1952). 306' 6" high. *(Skidmore, Owings and Merrill)*
F. *Mies van der Rohe* (1886   ). New York, Seagram Building (1958). 520' high. *(A. A. Schechter Assoc.)*

A

B

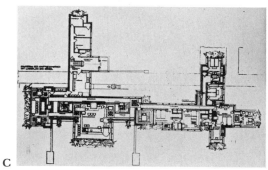

C

D

A. *Wright* (1869–1958). Oak Park, Ill., Unity Church (1906). 66′ x 66′ x 45′ high. *(MOMA)*
B. Oak Park, Unity Church. *(MOMA)*
C. *Wright.* Riverside, Ill., Coonley House (1908). *(Stoedtner)*
D. Riverside, Coonley House.

A. *Wright* (1869–1958). Pasadena, Millard Residence (1923). *(Stoedtner)*
B. *Wright.* Bear Run, Pa. Kaufmann House (1937–1939). *c.* 64′ x 62′. *(MOMA)*
C. *Wright.* Racine, Wis., Johnson Wax Company Building, tower (1947–1950). 153′ high. *(Wayne Andrews)*
D. *Wright.* New York, Guggenheim Museum (1957–1959). 100′ high to top of dome. *(Wayne Andrews)*

A

B

C

D

A. *Stone* (1902–   ). New Delhi, U. S. Embassy, from model (1959). 133′ wide. *(U.S. Dept. of State)*
B. *Stone*. Brussels, World's Fair, U.S. Pavilion (1958). 430′ diameter. *(U.S. Dept. of State)*
C. *Saarinen* (1910–1961). Cambridge, Kresge Auditorium (1955). 160′ span x 50′ high. *(Wayne Andrews)*
D. *Candela* (1910–   ). Xochimilco, Los Manantiales Restaurant (1958). 34′ high. *(Pan Am., photo Erwin Lang)*

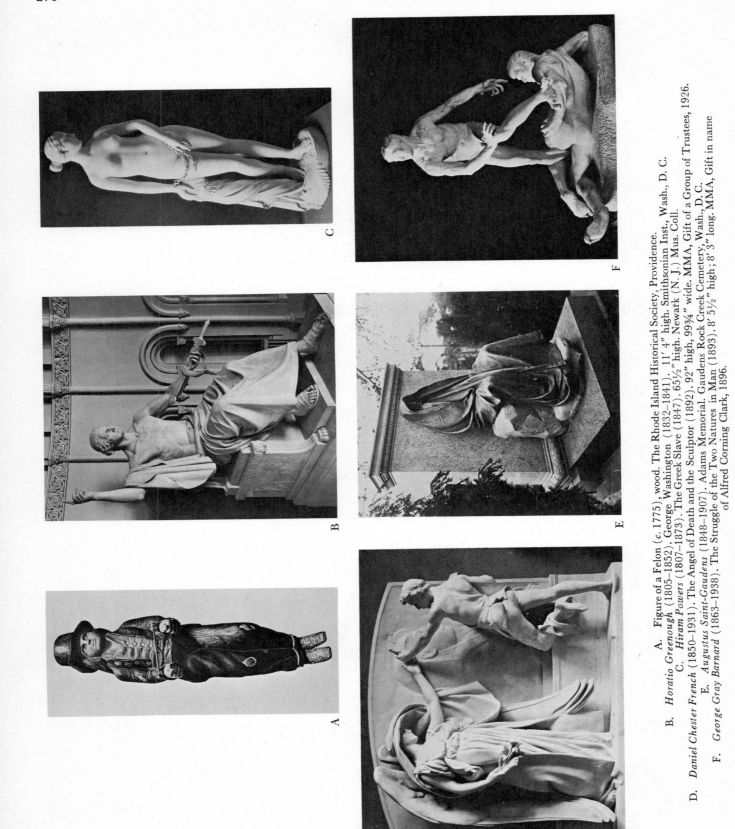

A.   Figure of a Felon (*c.* 1775), wood. The Rhode Island Historical Society, Providence.

B.   *Horatio Greenough* (1805–1852). George Washington (1832–1841). 11' 4" high. Smithsonian Inst., Wash., D. C.

C.   *Hiram Powers* (1807–1873). The Greek Slave (1847). 65½" high. Newark (N. J.) Mus. Coll.

D.   *Daniel Chester French* (1850–1931). The Angel of Death and the Sculptor (1892). 92" high, 99¾" wide. MMA, Gift of a Group of Trustees, 1926.

E.   *Augustus Saint-Gaudens* (1848–1907). Adams Memorial. Gaudens Rock Creek Cemetery, Wash., D. C.

F.   *George Gray Barnard* (1863–1938). The Struggle of the Two Natures in Man (1893). 8' 5½" high; 8' 3" long. MMA, Gift in name of Alfred Corning Clark, 1896.

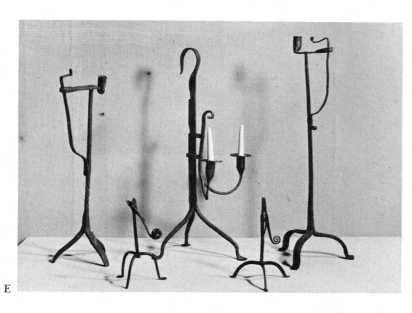

A. *William Zorach* (1887–   ). Head of Christ (1940). 14¾″ high. MOMA, Mrs. John D. Rockefeller, Jr., Fund.
B. *Gaston Lachaise* (1882–1935). John Marin (1928). 12½″ high. MOMA, Gift of Mrs. John D. Rockefeller, Jr.
C. *John B. Flannagan* (1895–1942). Triumph of the Egg, I (1937). 16″ long. MOMA.
D. *Jacques Lipchitz* (1891–   ). Figure (1926–1930). 7′ 1¼″ high. MOMA, van Gogh Purchase Fund.
E. Candlesticks (1720–1750). Art Inst., Chicago.
F. *Isamu Noguchi* (1904–   ). Unknown Bird (1949). 57″ high. Courtesy of the artist.

A

B

D

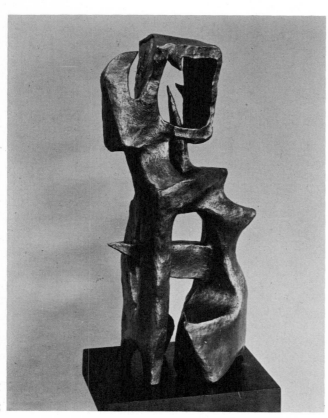

C

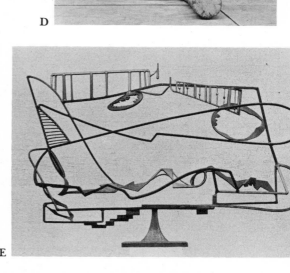

E

A. *Richard Lippold* (1915–   ). Variation No. 7: Full Moon (1949-1950). 10′ high. MOMA, Mrs. Simon Guggenheim Fund.
B. *Alexander Calder* (1898–   ). Lobster Trap and Fish Tail (1939). 8½′ high. MOMA, Gift of Advisory Committee.
C. *Seymour Lipton* (1903–   ). Cerberus (1947). 23″ high. Parsons Gal., New York. *(Walter J. Russell)*
D. *Alexander Calder.* Whale (1937). 6′ 6″ high. MOMA, Gift of the artist.
E. *David Smith* (1906–   ). Hudson River Landscape (1951). 75″ long. Whitney Mus. Am. Art, N. Y. *(Oliver Baker)*

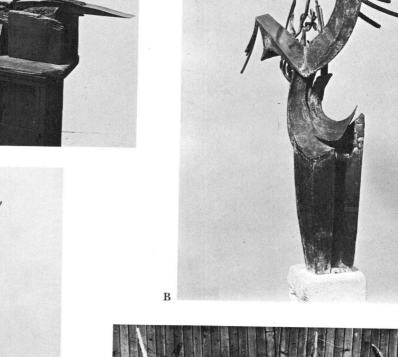

A. *Louise Nevelson* (1900–   ). Formation IV (1956). *(Courtesy of the artist)*
B. *Julio Gonzales* (1908–   ). Woman Combing Her Hair (1936). 52″ high. MOMA, Mrs. Simon Guggenheim Fund.
C. *David Hare* (1917–   ). Fruit Tree (1956). 5′ 4″ high. Joseph H. Hirshhorn Coll., New York. *(Kootz Gal.)*
D. *Theodore J. Roszak* (1907–   ). Spectre of Kitty Hawk (1946-1947). 40¼″ high. MOMA.
E. *Herbert Ferber* (1906–   ). Burning Bush (1951). 12′ 8″ x 7′ 10″. Congregation B'Nai Israel, Milburn, N. J.

A

C

B

D

E

F

A.　*Robert Feke* (1705?–1750?). Self-portrait (1749–1750). 50″ x 40″. Courtesy of the Rhode Island Historical Society.
B.　*Ralph Earl* (1751–1801). Roger Sherman (1775–1777). 64⅝″ x 49⅝″. Yale Univ. Art Gal., Gift of Robert Sherman White.
C.　*John Singleton Copley* (1737–1815). The Copley Family. 72½″ x 90⅜″. National Gallery of Art Purchase Fund, Andrew W. Mellon gift. Nat. Gal. Art, Washington, D. C.
D.　*Ralph Earl.* Looking East from Denny Hill. 45¾″ x 79⅜″. Worcester (Mass.) Art Mus.
E.　*John Singleton Copley.* Portrait of Paul Revere. (*c.* 1765–1770). 37⅞″ x 28½″. MFA.
F.　*Benjamin West* (1738–1820). Penn's Treaty with the Indians. 75½″ x 108¾″. Pa. Acad. Fine Arts, Phila.

A. *John Singleton Copley* (1737–1815). Mrs. Thomas Boylston. 50½″ x 40½″. (1776). Fogg.
B. *Gilbert Stuart* (1755–1828). Mrs. Richard Yates. 30¼″ x 25″. Nat. Gal., Wash., Mellon Coll., 1940.
C. *John Singleton Copley.* Watson and the Shark (1778). 72½″ x 90¼″. MFA.
D. *Gilbert Stuart.* The Skater. 96⅝″ x 58⅛″. Nat. Gal., Wash.
E. *John Trumbull* (1756–1843). Capture of the Hessians at Trenton (1786–1797). 19⅞″ x 30″. Yale Univ. Art. Gal.
F. *Thomas Sully* (1783–1872). Queen Victoria (1838). 36″ x 28¼″. MMA, Bequest of Francis T. S. Darley, 1914.

A.   *Washington Allston* (1779–1843). Moonlit Landscape (1819). 24″ x 35″. MFA.

B.   *John Vanderlyn* (1776–1852). Ariadne of Naxos (1814). 68″ x 87″. Pa. Acad. Fine Arts. *(Phillips Studio)*

C.   *John Greenwood* (1727–1792). Sea Captains Carousing in Surinam (1757–1758). 37¾″ x 75¼″. City Art Mus., St. Louis.

D.   *John Quidor* (1801–1881). Rip Van Winkle at Nicholas Vedder's Tavern (1839). 27¼″ x 34¼″. MFA, M. and M. Karolik Coll.

E.   *Thomas Cole* (1801–1848). The Oxbow of the Connecticut (1836). 51½″ x 76″. MMA, Gift of Mrs. Russell Sage, 1908.

F.   *Thomas Cole.* Expulsion from the Garden of Eden (1828). 39″ x 54″. MFA, M. and M. Karolik Coll.

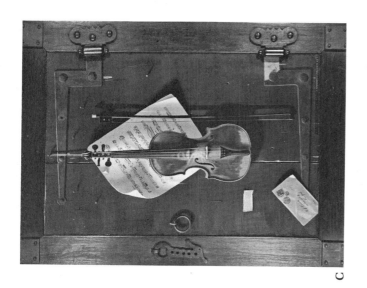

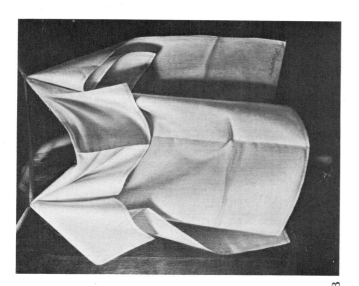

A. *Charles W. Peale* (1741–1847). Staircase Group (*c.* 1795). 89″ x 39½″. Phila. Mus. Art, George W. Eakins Coll.
B. *Raphael Peale* (1774–1825). After the Bath (1823). 29″ x 24″. Nelson Gal.–Atkins Mus. (Nelson Fund)
C. *William M. Harnett* (1848–1892). The Old Violin (1886). Lithographic Reproduction by Gus Ilg, 1887, with frame continuing picture in three dimensions, 42¾″ x 31¾″. Phila. Mus. Art.
D. *Thomas Chambers* (19th century). Looking North to Kingston. 22½″ x 30″. Smith College Mus. Art, Northampton, Mass.
E. *William Sidney Mount* (1807–1868). Eel Spearing at Setauket (1845). 29″ x 36″. N. Y. State Hist. Assn., Cooperstown.

A

B

C

D

E

F

A. *Erastus Salisbury Field* (1805–1900). Historical Monument of the American Republic (*c.* 1876). 9′ 7″ x 13′ 1″. Courtesy of the Morgan Wesson Mem. Coll., Mus. Fine Arts, Springfield, Mass.

B. *Albert Bierstadt* (1830–1902). Rocky Mountains (1863). 73¼″ x 120¾″. MMA, Rogers Fund, 1907.

C. *George Caleb Bingham* (1811–1879). Fur Traders Descending the Missouri (*c.* 1845). 29″ x 36½″. MMA, Morris K. Jesup Fund, 1933.

D. *George Inness* (1825–1894). Peace and Plenty (1865). 77⅝″ x 112⅜″. MMA, Gift of George A. Hearn, 1894.

E. *Ralph Blakelock* (1847–1919). Moonlight. 27¼″ x 32¼″. The Brooklyn Mus.

F. *Martin Johnson Heade* (1819–1903). Approaching Storm, Beach near Newport. 28″ x 57″. MFA, M. and M. Karolik Coll.

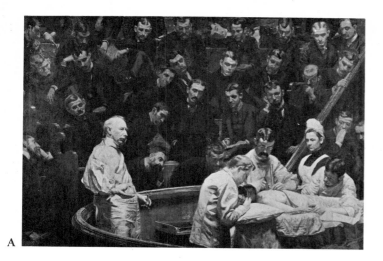

A.   *Thomas Eakins* (1844–1916). The Agnew Clinic (1889). 74½″ x 130½″. Univ. of Pa., Phila.
B.   *Thomas Eakins.* Walt Whitman (1887). 30″ x 24″. Pa. Acad. Fine Arts.
C.   *Thomas Eakins.* John Bigler in Single Scull (*c.* 1874). 24-5/16″ x 16″. Yale Univ. Art Gal., Whitney Coll. Sport Art.
D.   *Thomas Eakins.* Sailing (1874). 32″ x 46⅜″. Phila. Mus. Art.
E.   *John Singer Sargent* (1865–1925). El Jaleo. 7′ 7¼″ x 11′ 5″. Gardner Mus., Boston.
F.   *John Singer Sargent.* Madame X (Madame Gautreau). 82⅛″ x 43¼″. MMA, Arthur H. Hearn Fund, 1916.

B

D

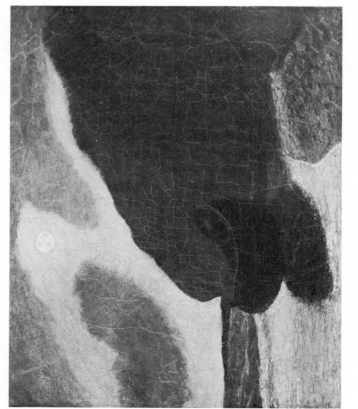

C

A

A. *Albert Pinkham Ryder* (1847–1917). Death on a Pale Horse (The Racetrack). 28¼″ x 35¼″. Cleveland Mus. Art, Purchase
from J. H. Wade Fund.
B. *Albert Pinkham Ryder*. Dead Bird (1890–1900). 4¼″ x 9⅞″. Phillips Coll.
C. *Albert Pinkham Ryder*. Moonlit Cove (1890–1900). 14″ x 17″. Phillips Coll.
D. *Albert Pinkham Ryder*. Siegfried and the Rhine Maidens (exhib'd 1891). 19⅞″ x 20½″. Nat. Gal, Wash, Mellon Coll., 1945.

A.   *Winslow Homer* (1836–1910). Hurricane, Bahamas (1898). 14½″ x 21″. MMA, Lazarus Fund, 1910.
B.   *Winslow Homer*. Saguenay River, Lower Rapids. 14″ x 20⅛″. Worcester (Mass.) Art Mus.
C. *Winslow Homer*. Coast in Winter. 28⅜″ x 48⅜″. Worcester Art Mus., Theodore T. and Mary G. Ellis Coll.
D.   *Winslow Homer*. Right and Left. 28¼″ x 48⅜″. Nat. Gal., Wash., Gift of Avalon Fund.
Page   E.   *Arthur B. Davies* (1862–1928). Along the Erie Canal. 18″ x 40″ Phillips Coll.
F.   *Louis Michel Eilshemius* (1864–1941). Afternoon Wind (1899). 20″ x 36″. MOMA.

A

B

C

D

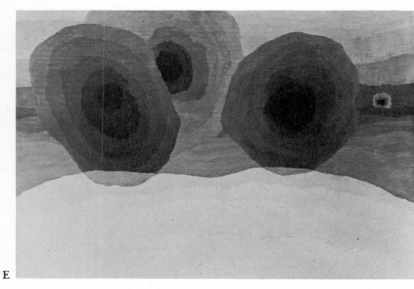

E

F

A.   *Maurice Prendergast* (1859–1924). The East River (1901). 13¾″ x 19¾″. MOMA, Gift of Mrs. John D. Rockefeller, Jr.
B.   *George B. Luks* (1867–1933). Otis Skinner as Col. Bridau (1919). 52″ x 44″. Phillips Coll.
C.   *Charles Demuth* (1883–1935). My Egypt (1925). 36″ x 30″. Coll. Whitney Mus. Am. Art, New York.
D.   *John Sloan* (1871–1951). The Wake of the Ferry (1907). 26″ x 32″. Phillips Coll.
E.   *Arthur G. Dove* (1880–1946). Fog-horns (1929). 20″ x 28″. Colorado Springs Fine Arts Cent.
F.   *Arthur G. Dove*. Flour Mill Abstraction (1938). 26″ x 16″. Phillips Coll.

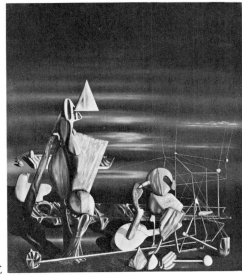

A. *George W. Bellows* (1882–1925). Both Members of This Club (1909). 45¼″ x 63⅛″. Nat. Gal., Wash., Gift of Chester Dale.
B. *Walt Kuhn* (1880–1949). Juggler. 30″ x 25″. Nelson Gal., Gift of Friends of Art.
C. *Max Ernst* (1891–   ). Forest (1926). 28¾″ x 36¼″. MOMA.
D. *Max Weber* (1881–   ). The Geranium (1911). 39⅞″ x 32¼″. MOMA, Lillie P. Bliss Coll.
E. *Ives Tanguy* (1900–1955). Slowly toward the North (1942). 42″ x 36″. MOMA, Gift of Philip C. Johnson.
F. *Salvador Dali* (1904–   ). Paranoic Astral Image (1934). 6¼″ x 8¹¹⁄₁₆″. Wadsworth Atheneum, Hartford, Conn.

A

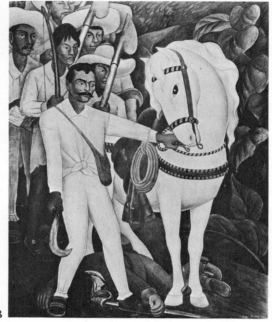

B

C

D

E

A.   *José Clemente Orozco* (1883–1949). Cortez and the Cross, and the Machine (1932–1934). 10 ′ 6″ x 24′ 10″. By permission of the
Trustees of Dartmouth College, Hanover, N. H.
B.   *Diego Rivera* (1886–1957). Agrarian Leader Zapata (1931). 93¾″ x 74″. MOMA, Commissioned by
Mrs. John D. Rockefeller, Jr., 1931.
C.   *Jack Levine* (1915–   ). Feast of Pure Reason (1937). 42″ x 48″. MOMA, loan from United States WPA Art Program.
D.   *Thomas Hart Benton* (1889–   ). Arts of the West (1932). 8″ x 13″. New Britain (Conn.) Mus. Am. Art.
E.   *Ben Shahn* (1898–   ). The Passion of Sacco and Vanzetti (1931–1932). 84½″ x 48″. Coll. Whitney Mus. Am. Art, Gift of Edith
and Milton Loewenthal in Memory of Juliana Force.

A. *Grant Wood* (1892–1942). Daughters of Revolution. 40″ x 20″. Cincinnati Art. Mus.
B. *Reginald Marsh* (1898–1954). Why Not Use the "L"? 36″ x 48″. Coll. Whitney Mus. Am. Art.
C. *Stephen Greene* (1918–   ). The Burial (1947). 42″ x 55″. Coll. Whitney Mus. Am. Art.
D. *Yasuo Kuniyoshi* (1893–1953). Amazing Juggler. 65″ x 40¼″. Des Moines (Iowa) Art Cent., Edmundson Coll.
E. *Alton Pickens* (1917–   ). Carnival (1949). 54⅝″ x 40⅜″. MOMA, Gift of Lincoln Kirstein.
F. *Andrew Wyeth* (1917–   ). Christina's World (1948). 32¼″ x 47¾″. MOMA., Purchase.

C

F

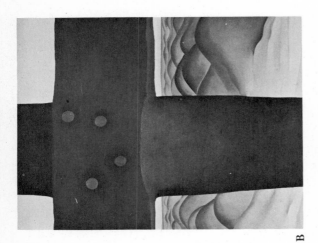

B

E

A

D

A. *Stanton McDonald-Wright* (1890–   ). Conception Synchromy (1915). 30″ x 24″. Coll. Whitney Mus. Am. Art, Gift of George F. Of.
B. *Georgia O'Keeffe* (1887–   ). Black Cross, New Mexico (1929). 39″ x 30-1/16″. Art. Inst., Chicago.
C. *Arthur B. Carles* (1882–1952). Composition III (1931–1932). 51⅜″ x 38¾″. MOMA, Gift of Leopold Stokowski.
D. *Karl Knaths* (1891–   ). Maritime. 40″ x 30″. Phillips Coll.
E. *Josef Albers* (1888–   ). Homage to the Square – Precinct (1951). 31¾″ x 31¾″. MMA, George A. Hearn Fund, 1953.
F. *Stuart Davis* (1894–   ). Owh! In San Pao (1951). 52¼″ x 41¾″. Coll. Whitney Mus. Am. Art.

A   B

C   D

E   F

A. *Joseph Stella* (1877–1946). The Bridge, No. 5 of five panels, "New York Interpreted." 88¼" x 54". Newark (N. J.) Mus.
B. *Edward Hopper* (1882–   ). House by the Railroad (1925). 24" x 29". MOMA.
C. *Charles F. Burchfield* (1893–   ). Sun and Rocks. 40" x 56". Albright Art Gal.
D. *Charles Sheeler* (1883–   ). The Artist Looks at Nature (1943). 21" x 18". Art Inst., Chicago, Gift of the Society for Contemporary Am. Art.
E. *William Baziotes* (1912–1963). Dwarf (1947). 42" x 36⅛". MOMA, A. Conger Goodyear Fund.
F. *Theodore Stamos* (1922–   ). Sounds in the Rock (1946). 48⅛" x 28⅜". MOMA, Gift of Edward W. Root.

A. *Marsden Hartley* (1877–1943). Mt. Katahdin, Autumn, No. 1. 30″ x 40″. Univ. of Nebraska, F. M. Hall Coll.
B. *John Marin* (1870–1953). Off Cape Split, Maine. 22⅛″ x 28⅛″. MMA, George A. Hearn Fund, 1946.
C. *Marsden Hartley.* Nova Scotia Fishermen (1938). 30″ x 40″. IBM Corp. Coll.
D. *John Marin.* Maine Islands (1922). 16¾″ x 20″. Phillips Coll.
E. *Morris Graves* (1910–   ). Blind Bird (1940). 30⅛″ x 27″. MOMA.
F. *Mark Tobey* (1890–   ). Edge of August (1953). 48″ x 28″. MOMA.

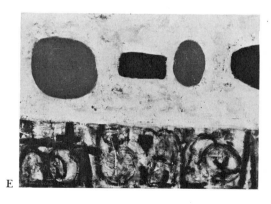

A.   *Arshile Gorky* (1904–1948). The Betrothal, II (1947). 50¾″ x 38″. Coll. Whitney Mus. Am. Art.
B.   *Hans Hofmann* (1880–   ). Embrace (1947). 23¾″ x 57″. Lane Coll., Leominster, Mass.
C.   *Bradley Walker Tomlin* (1899–1953). No. 9: In Praise of Gertrude Stein (1950). 49″ x 102½″. MOMA, Gift of Mrs. John D. Rockefeller, Jr.
D.   *Matta,* or *Sebastian Antonio Matta Echaurren* (1912). Listen to Living (1941). 29½″ x 37⅜″. MOMA, N. Y. Inter-Am. Fund.
E.   *Adolph Gottlieb* (1903). Frozen Sounds II (1952). 36″ x 48″. Albright Art Gal., Gift of Seymour H. Knox.

A. *Clyfford Still* (1904–   ). Painting (1951). 7′ 10″ x 6′ 10″. MOMA, Blanchette Rockefeller Fund.
B. *Jackson Pollock* (1912–1956). Ocean Grayness (1953). 57¾″ x 90⅛″. Guggenheim Mus.
C. *Mark Rothko* (1903–   ). Number 10 (1950). 90⅜″ x 57⅛″. MOMA, Gift of Philip C. Johnson.
D. *Jackson Pollock*. Blue Poles (1952). 6′ 11″ x 16′ 1″. Sidney Janis Gal., N. Y.
E. *Robert Motherwell* (1915–   ). The Voyage (1949). 48″ x 94″. MOMA, Gift of Mrs. John D. Rockefeller, III.

A.   *Joan Mitchell* (1929–   ). Hemlock (1956). 91″ x 80″. Whitney Mus.
B.   *Philip Guston* (1912–   ). The Sleeper (1958). 66¼″ x 76″. Fairweather-Hardin Gal., Chicago.
C.   *Sam Francis* (1923–   ). Red in Red (1955). 78¾″ x 78½″. Martha Jackson Gal.
D.   *Fritz Bultman* (1919–   ). Sleeper No. 2 (1952). 30″ x 38″. Whitney Mus.
E.   *Jack Tworkov* (1900–   ). Dedicated to Stephan Wolfe (1960). 88″ x 75″. Michener Found. Coll., Allentown, Pa.

A.   *Franz Kline* (1910–1962). Initial (1959). 8′ 4½″ x 6′ 5½″. Sidney Janis Gal. *(Oliver Baker)*
B.   *Franz Kline.* Cross-section (1956). 53¼″ x 63½″. Sidney Janis Gal. *(Oliver Baker)*
C.   *Willem de Kooning* (1904–   ). Woman and Bicycle (1952–1953). 76½″ x 49″. Whitney Mus. *(Oliver Baker)*
D.   *Willem de Kooning.* February (1957). 79″ x 69″. Janis Gal., Dr. and Mrs. Edgar Berman Coll. *(Oliver Baker)*

A.   Uxmal, Temple of the Magician (700–1000). 160′ x 240′ x 80′ high. *(Pan Am.)*
B.   Uxmal, The Nunnery (700–1000). 189′ x 33′ 6″.
C.   Chichen Itzá, Las Monjas (950–1150). 104′ x 30′. *(Pan Am.)*
D.   Chichen Itzá, El Castillo (950–1150). 102′ high. *(Pan Am., Barbachan Trav. Service)*
E.   Tampumachy, stone architecture, detail (1438–1532).
F.   Arizona, Montezuma's Castle (1102–1121). EMU.
G.   Taos. Pueblo (*c.* 1540). *(Santa Fe Ry.)*

A   B   C

D   E   F

A.   Peruvian Water Jug, Mochica (*c.* 650 A.D.). 11½″ high. Courtesy, Prof. W. D. Strong.
B.   Peruvian Water Jug, Nazca (700–1000). 6″ high. Courtesy, Prof. W. D. Strong.
C.   Silver Alpaca, Inca (*c.* 1400–1500). *c.* 8″ high. Am. Mus. Nat. Hist.
D.   Stone Figure, Stela Bennett, Tiahuanaco (1000–1300). *c.* 24′ high. Am. Mus. Nat. Hist.
E.   Stela, Copán, Classic Maya (450–550). Mus. de l'Homme.
F.   Stela 14, Piedras Negras, Classic Maya (450–550). *c.* 9′ high. Univ. Mus., Philadelphia.

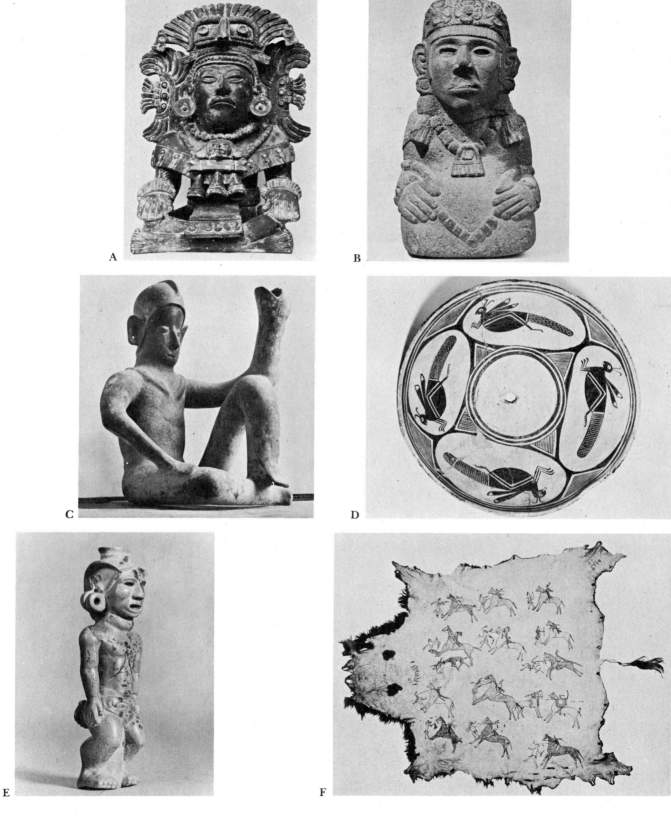

A. Anthropomorphic Urn, Monte Alban–Zapotec (500–1000). 26½″ high. Mus. Am. Indian, N. Y.
B. Stone Figure, Aztec (1325–1521). 13½″ high. Courtesy of The Mus. Prim Art. N. Y.
C. Figure with Arm Raised, Tarasca (c. 1200). 14″ high. Coll. Diego Rivera.
D. Pottery Bowl, Mimbres (950–1050). Buffalo Soc. Nat. Sci. *(Photo C. E. Simmons)*
E. Figure, Hopewell Culture (A.D. 500?). Ohio State Mus., Columbus.
F. Painted Buffalo Robe, Dakota (19th century). 9′ x 7′ 6″. Am. Mus. Nat. Hist.

A.   Victoria, House of the Three Tribes—Nootka, Haida, Salish. *(Canadian Nat. Rys.)*
B.   Tlingit Robe. Linden Mus., Stuttgart. *(Stoedtner)*
C.   Benin King (19th century). 17½″ high. Univ. Mus., Philadelphia.
D.   Figure, Dogon, West Africa (19th century). 23″ high. Univ. Mus., Philadelphia.
E.   Figure, Baoulé, West Africa (19th century). 18½″ high. Royal Scottish Mus., Edinburgh. *(P. S. Wingert)*
F.   Figure, Yoruba, West Africa (19th century). 14½″ high. Brit. Mus. *(P. S. Wingert)*

A

B

C

D

E

F

A. Mask, Ibo, West Africa (19th century?). 17¾" high. Courtesy of The Mus. Prim. Art. *(Charles Uht)*
B. Mask, Cameroons, West Africa (19th century). 20" high. Linden Mus., Stuttgart. *(P. S. Wingert)*
C. Figure, Western Congo, Central Africa (19th century). 10¾" high. In the Brooklyn Mus. Coll.
D. Fang, Gabon, Central Africa (19th century?). 22½" high. Courtesy of The Mus. Prim. Art. *(Charles Uht)*
E. Mask, Sepik River, New Guinea (19th–20th centuries). 22" high. Amer. Mus. Nat. Hist.
F. Mask, New Britain (19th century). 42" high. Courtesy Denver Art. Mus. Coll.

A.   Figure, Hawaii (late 18th–early 19th centuries). 43½″ high. Bishop Mus., Honolulu. *(P. S. Wingert)*
B.   Maori House, New Zealand (19th century). *(Stoedtner)*
C.   Maori House Panel, New Zealand (1842–1843). 6′ 6″ high. Dominion Mus., Wellington. *(P. S. Wingert)*
D.   Canoe Prow Figure, Solomon Islands (19th century). 8½″ high. Mus. für Völkerkunde, Hamburg. *(P.S. Wingert)*
E.   Stone Figure, Marquesas (early 19th century). 8″ high. Univ. Mus., Philadelphia.
F.   Stone Figure, Easter Island (late 18th–early 19th centuries). Brit. Mus. *(Stoedtner)*

A.   Torso from Harappa (*c.* 3000 B.C.). Archaeolog. Mus., Mohenjo-Daro. (© *Archaeolog. Survey of India*)

B.   Sanchi, Stupa No. 1 (70–25 B.C.). 120′ diameter, x 54′ high. (*GITO*)

C.   Asokan Capital (322–185 B.C.). 7′ x 2′ 10″. Archaeolog. Mus., Sarnath. (© *Archaeolog. Survey of India*)

D.   Yakshi, East Gate, Stupa No. 1, Sanchi (70–25 B.C.). (*Henry Janson*)

E.   Karli, Chaitya Hall (185–80 B.C.). 124′ long x 45′ high. (*Johnston and Hoffman*)

F.   Buddha Preaching in the Deer Park (A.D. 320–600). 5′ 3″ high. Archaeolog. Mus., Sarnath. (*GITO*)

A.   Bodhisattva Dedicated by Friar Bala (A.D. 131–132). 8′ 2″ high. Archaeolog. Mus., Sarnath. *(B. Rowland)*
B.   Ajanta, Cave XIX (320–600). 32′ wide x 38′ high. *(Johnston and Hoffman)*
C.   Colossal Buddha, Bamian (5th century). 175′ high. *(B. Rowland)*
D.   The Beautiful Bodhisattva, detail, Cave I, Ajanta (320–600). Complete fresco, 5′ 10″ high. *(GITO)*
E.   Saiva Trinity, Hindu Temple, Elephanta (8th century). 12′ high. *(GITO, photo Johnston and Hoffman)*
F.   Dancing Siva (13th century). 3′ 11″ high. Courtesy Gov. Mus., Madras.

A.   Aihole, Durga Temple (320–600). 84′ x 36′ x 30′ high. (© *Archaeolog. Survey of India*)
B.   Bodhgaya, Mahabodhi Temple, restored (4th century). 180′ high.
C.   Elura, Kailasa Temple (600–850). 200′ x 100′ x 100′ high. (*India Of., London*)
D.   Konarak, Surya Temple, Black Pagoda, wheel (13th century). 10′ high. (*Johnston and Hoffman*)
E.   Madura, Great Temple, Gopuram (17th century). *c.* 200′ high. (*B. Rowland*)

A.   Mt. Abu, Jain Temple (11th–12th centuries). *(Johnston and Hoffman)*
B.   Buddha Nirvana with Ananda, Gal Vihara, Polonnaruva (13th century). 23′ high. *(Paul Popper, Ltd.)*
C.   Barabudur, Great Stupa (8th century). 100′ high. *(Mil. Intell. Serv., Batavia)*
D.   The Bayon, Angkor Thom (1112–1152). Face, 9′ high. *(Cambodian Embassy)*
E.   Angkor Vat (12th century). Central tower, 200′ high. *(W. F. Barden)*

[1] For Islamic Art of India, see Plate 59.

A. Owl, from Anyang (1400–1100 B.C.). 17¾″ high. Academica Sinica, Nanking.
B. Tripod Vessel, Type Ting (1400–1100 B.C.). 9½″ high. Art Inst., Chicago.
C. Wine Vessel, Type Chüeh (1400–900 B.C.). 10″ x 9″. Freer.
D. Beaker, Type Ku (12th century B.C.). 11″ x 6¼″. Courtesy of the Nelson Gal. of Art and Atkins Mus., Kansas City. (Nelson Fund)
E. Bell, Type Chung (600–250 B.C.). Stoclet Collection, Brussels. (M. A. Stoclet)
F. Nankow, Great Wall (3rd century B.C.). (Stoedtner)
G. Bear (2nd century B.C.–A.D. 2nd century). 6¼″ x 8¼″. Gardner Mus., Boston.
H. Horse Trampling Barbarian Warrior, Tomb of Ho Ch'ü-ping, Shensi (117 B.C.). 6′ 3″ x 5′ 4″. (Mus. Guimet, photo Victor Segalen)
I. House Model (A.D. 2nd century). 4′ 4″ high. Courtesy Nelson Gal. and Atkins Mus.

A.   Visit of Mu Wang to Hsi Wang Mu, Tomb of Wo Liang Tzu, Shantung (2nd century). *(Fogg)*
B.   Colossal Buddha, Yunkang (5th century). 32' high. *(Iwata)*
C.   Empress as Donor, Pin Yang Cave, Lungmen (6th century). 6' 4" x 9' 1". *(Nelson Gal. and Atkins Mus.)*
D.   Colossal Vairocana Buddha, Lungmen (672–676). 85' high. *(Iwata)*
E.   Guardians, Lungmen (672–676). 50' high. *(Nelson Gal. and Atkins Mus., photo L. Sickman)*

A

B

C

D

A. *Ku K'ai-chih* (*c.* 350–400). Admonitions of the Imperial Preceptress. 10″ high. Brit. Mus.
B. Amitabha Paradise, Cave 139A, Tunhuang (9th century). *(Mus. Guimet, photo Paul Pelliot)*
C. Adoring Buddha, from Tunhuang (8th century). 4′ high. Fogg.
D. *Tung Yuan* (10th century). Clear Weather in the Valley, detail. 1′ 3″ high. MFA.

A. *Fan K'uan* (*fl.* 990–1030). A Temple among the Snowy Hills. 10″ x 10″. MFA.
B. *Hui Tsung* (1082–1135). The Five-colored Parakeet. 21″ high. MFA.
C. *Mi Fei* (1051–1107). Misty Landscape. 4′ 11″ x 2′ 7″. Freer.
D. *Hsia Kuei* (*fl.* 1195–1224). Rain Storm. Baron Kawasaki Coll., Kobe.
E. *Liang K'ai* (*fl.* 12th century). The Priest Hui-neng. 2′ 6″ high. Count Matsudaira Coll., Tokyo.

A

B

C

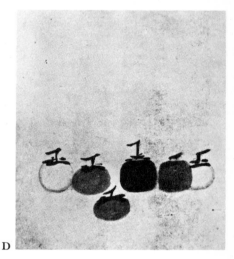

D

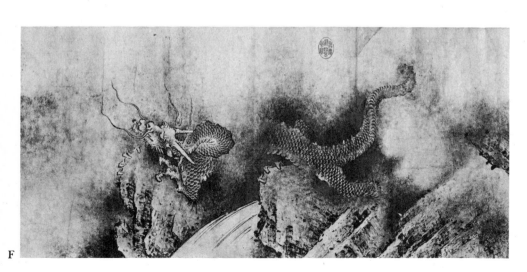

F

E

A.   *Li T'ang* (*fl.*1100–1130). Man on a Water Buffalo. 10″ x 11″. MFA.
B.   *Ma Lin* (*fl.* 1215–1225). Ling Chao-nü Standing in the Snow. 9½″ x 10″. MFA.
C.   *Ma Fen* (*fl.* 11th century). Hundred Geese Scroll, detail. 1′ 2″ high. Acad. Arts, Honolulu.
D.   *Mu Ch'i* (13th century). Persimmons. 14″ x 15″. Ryukoin Temple, Kyoto.
E.   *Lu Hsin-chung* (13th century). Vanavasi Gazing at a Lotus Pond. 3′ 8″ x 1′ 4″. MFA.
F.   *Ch'en Jung* (*fl.* 1235–1255). Nine Dragon Scroll, detail. 1′ 6″ high. MFA.

A

B

C

D

E

F

A.   *Kuan Tao-sheng* (14th century). Bamboo (1309). 11″ x 4′ 6″. MFA.
B.   *Ni Tsan* (1301–1374). Landscape (1362). 1′ x 1′ 8″. Freer.
C.   *Yen Hui.* An Immortal. Chion-ji, Kyoto.
D.   Peking, Palace, Grand Ancestral Shrine (15th century). 210′ x 150′ x 90′ high.
E.   Peking, Summer Palace, Bridge. *(Stoedtner)*
F.   Peking, Altar of Heaven.

A. *Tai Chin* (*fl.* 1430–1450). Breaking Waves and Autumn Winds, detail. 1′ high. Freer.
B. *Chu Tuan* (*fl.* 16th century). Man and Boy in a Boat under Trees (1518). 4′ x 2′. MFA.
C. *Leng Mei* (18th century). Lady Walking on a Garden Terrace. 3′ 6″ x 1′ 10″. MFA.
D. Kwannon, Horyu-ji Temple (6th–7th centuries). 6′ high. *(S. Ogawa)*
E. Izumo, Shinto Shrine.
F. Toshodai-ji, Lecture Hall (8th century).

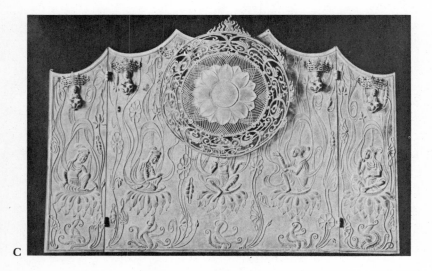

A.   Bodhisattva in Meditation, Chugu-ji Nunnery, Horyu-ji Temple (7th century). 5′ 2″ high. *(S. Ogawa)*
B.   Shrine of Lady Itachibana, Golden Hall, Horyu-ji Temple (7th century). *(S. Ogawa)*
C.   Screen and Halo, Shrine of Lady Itachibana, Screen, 1′ 9″ high; halo, 1′. *(S. Ogawa)*
D.   Nara, Yakushi-ji Temple, Pagoda (8th century). *(S. Ogawa)*
E.   Bonten, Hokkedo, Todai-ji Temple, Nara (8th century). 6′ 7″ high. *(S. Ogawa)*
F.   Yakushi, Yakushi-ji Temple, Nara (7th–8th tempuries). 7′ 4″ high. *(S. Ogawa)*

A.   The Priest Ganjin, Toshodai-ji Temple, Nara (8th century). 2′ 8″ high. *(S. Ogawa)*

B.   Uji, Byodoin Temple, Phoenix Hall (1053). *(Consulate Gen'l., Japan)*

C.   *Jocho* (*d.* 1057). Head of Amida, Byodoin Temple, Uji. Full figure, 9′ 8″ high. *(Stoedtner)*

D.   *Toba Sojo* (12th century). Hare Chasing a Monkey. 1′ high. Kozan-ji Temple, Kyoto.

E.   Kichijoten, Joruri-ji Temple, Kyoto (12th century). 2′ 11″ high. *(S. Ogawa)*

F.   Burning of the Sanjo Palace, detail (13th century). Complete scroll, 1′ 4″ x 22′ 11″. MFA.

A. *Unkei* (13th century). Hosso Patriarch Muchaku, detail (1208).Complete figure, 6′ 2″ high. Kofuku-ji Temple, Nara *(Stoedtner)*
B. **The Great Buddha**, Kamakura (1252). 42′ 6″ high. *(Japan Tour. Assn.)*
C. *Jokei* (13th century). Kongorikishi, Kofuku-ji Temple, Nara. *(S. Ogawa)*
D. Uesugi Shigefusa. Meigetsuin Temple, Kamakura (13th century). 2′ 3″ high.
E. *Koshun* (*fl.* 14th century). Hachiman as a Priest (1328). 32″ high. MFA.
F. Jizo (14th century). 33¼″ x 14½″. MMA, Gift of Mrs. J. Watson Webb, the H. O. Havemeyer Coll.

A.   *So-ami* (15th century). Chinese Landscape Screen (late 15th century). MMA, Gift of John D. Rockefeller, Jr., 1941.
B.   Kyoto, The Golden Pavilion (1397). *(Japan Tour Assn.)*
C.   *Sesshu* (1420–1506). Winter Landscape. 1′ 6″ x 1′. Manjuin Temple, Kyoto. *(Pageant of Japanese Art,* Vol. III, pl. 55)
D.   *Sesson* (16th century). Boat Returning in a Storm. 9″ x 12″. Nomura Tokushichi Coll., Osaka. *(Fogg)*
E.   Nagoya, Castle (1611). *(S. Ogawa)*
F.   Nikko, Toshogu Shrine, Yomeimon Gate (17th century). *(Japan Tour. Assn.)*

A

B

C

D

E

F

A. *Kiyomasu* (1679–1763). Actor Matsumoto Hyozo as a Woman (*c.* 1715). 21½″ x 12½″. MFA.
B. *Harunobu* (1725–1770). The Crow and the Heron. 11″ x 8″. MMA.
C. *Hokusai* (1760–1849). The Wave. 10″ x 15″. MFA.
D. *Utamaro* (1754–1806). Three Geisha. 14¾″ x 10″. Art Inst., Chicago.
E. *Sharaku* (18th century). Ichikawa Ebizo IV as Washizuka Kwandayu (1794). 14½″ x 9½″. MMA, Whittelsey Fund, 1949.
F. *Hiroshige* (1797–1858). Fifty-three Stages of the Tokaido: Shono (*c.* 1834). 9½″ x 14″. MFA.

INDEX